Picasso

bon vivant

Picasso

bon vivant

Ermine Herscher
in collaboration with Agnès Carbonell

Photography
Dennis Amon and Marianne Lemince

Photo Research
Janine Herscher

Recipe Styling
Josseline Rigot

RIZZOLI
NEW YORK

Picasso in 1955, photographed by Lartigue.

Contents

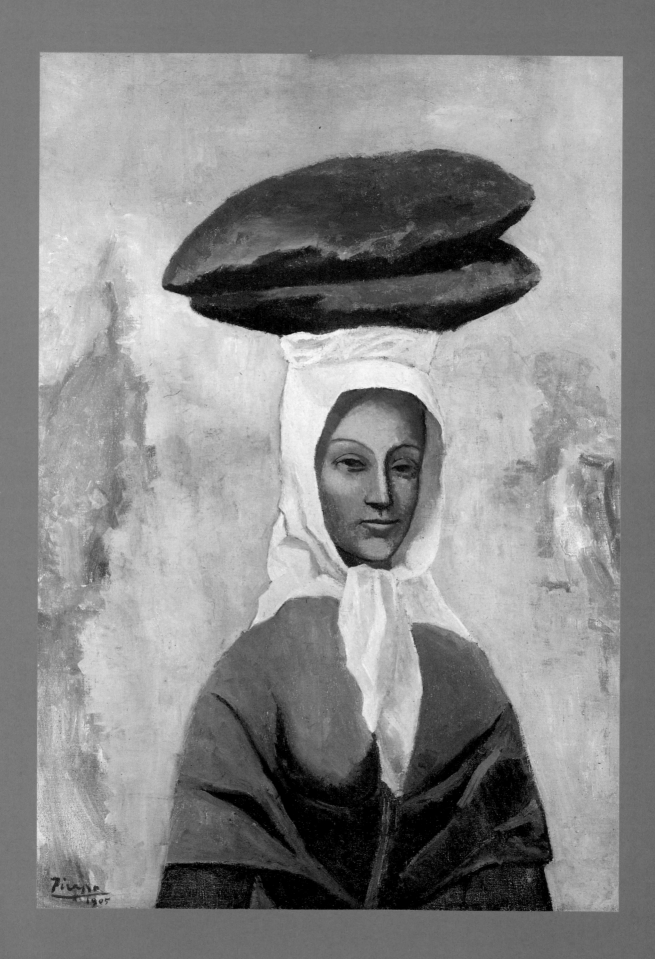

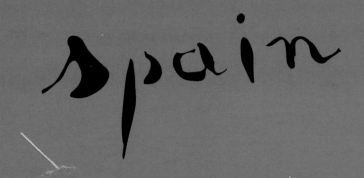

spain

Summer, 1898, Ports del Maestrat, in the southern Catalonia
mountains above Horta de Ebro.
Two young men set up camp in a

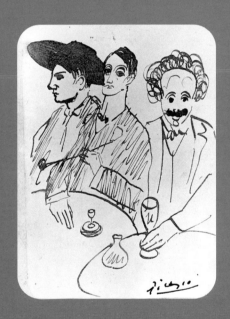

cave near the spring of a bubbling
mountain stream. One of them,
Manuel Pallarès, is the son of a pros-
perous farmer in Horta, a village situated two days walking distance

away. The other, coming from the city, is pale and gaunt. His name is Pablo Ruiz Picasso. These two friends met at the Barcelona Beaux-Arts four years earlier. Their shared passion for painting brings them closely together. They coat the walls of their cherished refuge in brilliant colors, they pile up mounds of grass for mattresses, and suspend their precious paints and painting supplies in tree branches. Pablo has even transported a large canvas on the back of a mule. The canvas is intended for a painting to be called *Idylle*, a tribute to their summer paradise. It is certainly a paradise for these two artists—replete with the roar of rushing waters and the combined fragrances of freshly cut grass and wood fires. They cook rice and chick peas carried up from Horta and, to improve upon their modest fare, they occasionally walk down to the nearest farm, the Mas del Quiquet, where they are given bread and game.

When Manuel's younger brother, Salvador, arrives with the canvases and frames Pablo has ordered, they feast on wild hare. The freshly killed animal is skinned and portioned, then roasted over red-hot embers. This setting reminds Pablo of the somber still lifes painted by his father, don José, an art professor at the Barcelona Beaux-Arts. Game, along with flowers and pigeons was one of his preferred subjects. But the hare Pablo was dining on that day had little to do with "furs and feathers," as he referred to his father's "paintings of partridges and pigeons, hares and rabbits that decorated dining rooms." In the wilderness and solitude of Ports del Maestrat, game takes on another meaning and flavor which will much later induce Picasso to say "Everything I know, I learned at the village of Pallarès."

*A*bove: *El Mas del Quiquet*, 1898, oil on canvas.

*P*age 8: *Woman carrying bread*, 1906, oil on canvas.

Picasso, with a large hat, and two members of the *tertulia:* Angel Fernandez de Soto, with whom he enjoyed wandering into the shady hotels of the Barrio Xino; and Sabastian Junyez, who owned *El Liberal*, the first newspaper to publish an article on a painting by Picasso.

Picasso's birthplace, 36 Plaza de la Merced, in Málaga. He was born October 25, 1881, at 11:15 pm. His childhood home is on the extreme left, behind the trees.

Lola cutting a cake, about 1899, pencil on paper. Lola, Picasso's sister, was his first model. "I drew her throughout the day, from rising in the morning to going to bed at night, helping my mother in the kitchen . . ."

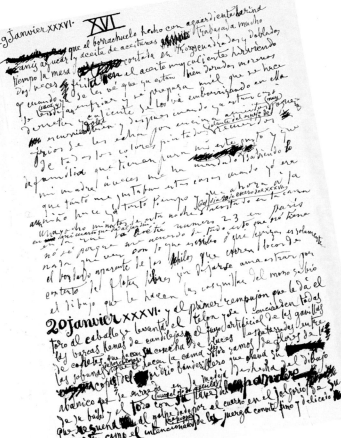

Above: *The kitchen*, 1896, oil on wood.
Opposite: Fragment of *Writings*, dated January 1936. Here Picasso gives the recipe for baba sprinkled with "little colored anise seeds," to which his mother treated him throughout his childhood.

In 1916, during one of the most difficult periods of his life, it was an image of the tiled kitchen from his childhood that Picasso drew in his declaration of love to Gaby, a neighbor at the time: "To help you forget your troubles look on the small dining room, I will be so happy to be with you . . ."

The Spanish Mountains

The Wild Life

Arriving in Horta de Ebro sickly and scrawny, Pablo quickly regained his health. Until now he had lived in whatever city his father's employment took the family—from Málaga l'Andalouse, where he was born on October 25, 1881, to La Corogne l'Atlantique, passing by Barcelona, dear to his heart, and Madrid, where he never fully adapted. It was in Horta that he finally discovered a universe that measured up to his appetite for life and creativity. He was the guest of Manuel's parents at Can Tafetans, one of the most beautiful homes in a fortified village set on top of a knoll. To reach the summit where their house was situated required a 25-mile (40 kilometers) hike through the mountains, crossing a roaring ford, and traversing the silence of the Hautes Terres that separated the Catalonia and Aragon regions.

Pablo earned a meager living by working in the fields. He also learned how to care for farm animals, harvest olives, and make olive oil in a press. Watching the oil ooze and trickle down from the press introduced Picasso to the ideology of the transformation of one element into another. The resulting olive oil is especially revered, as it is the basis of all Spanish cooking. A simple slab of bread rubbed with garlic and dipped in olive oil makes a noble snack. Picasso fondly remembers a dough made with olive oil, "kneaded for a long time, cut into small squares, and folded twice" which his mother used to make for him. These holiday beignets, called babas, are made with "eau de vie or brandy, flour, anise, sugar, and olive oil," and "fried in hot oil until well browned, then drained and cooled. Then they are rolled in

warmed, melted honey and when almost cool, sprinkled with small colored anise seeds." Though the holidays were religious events, they were not only occasions for processions and ceremonies, but also a pretext to drink and feast. Pablo prolonged his stay in Horta until February 1899, and joined in the festivities on All Saints Day and Epiphany, letting go of his temperate side to join in drink with the village.

But these excesses were rare. His customary meal was often limited to "a skillet full of eggs and 'taters," as he wrote in a surrealistic poem in 1959, portraying the humble life of a Spanish village. His diet included dried beans, a variety of sausages such as blood sausage, *boutifares,* and *sobresadas,* specialties of the country, to which he added yet more eggs and potatoes. And rice, above all there was rice. "Brown rice, white rice, buttered rice, plain rice, rice cooked in milk, rice soup." The list on how to prepare this modest starch was unending. In Horta, Pablo added yet another recipe to his repertoire on rice—gradually stir ladle after ladle of hot broth into a pan of slowly cooking rice. The rice takes on the flavor of the broth and each grain maintains its bite. With a pinch of saffron the rice is transformed into a dish of savory golden nuggets.

The young artist often used the color of saffron to enhance his landscape paintings. The yellows and pinks that bathe his painting *Mas del Quiquet* give the impression that he crushed a few of the perfumed threads directly onto his palette as he painted. His surrealistic poem, written in 1959, described the inhabitants of Horta. Among them were young girls and the parish priest, who were "amazed by the cold

above: *asas de Horta*, 1898–1899, study in pencil on album paper.

Following pages: *Catalonia Landscape.*

paints, the saffron and the strong green, the vermicelli and cotton black raisins [...]" The artist's allusions to food link his observations of reality to his particular perceptions. His style was never based on accommodating reality, a point made by cubism.

Catalonian Reunions

In the summer of 1906 Pablo set himself up in a unique inn in Gósol, a small village in the Pyrénées. He adopted his mother's surname, Picasso, and from then on used it to sign his paintings. In Gósol, the painter and his companion, Fernande Olivier, celebrated their return to the "wild life" far from the cities Picasso had lived in since his departure from Horta. Shortly after his arrival, Picasso was so transformed that the astonished Fernande could barely believe her eyes: "The Picasso I saw in Spain was completely different from the Picasso I knew in Paris; he was cheerful, less wild, more brilliant and animated, and able to interest himself in things in a calm and rational manner; he was actually at ease."

In this peaceful environment, the air "was extraordinarily pure." The location offered the advantage of robust and simple food, and was far from the picturesque, touristic "Spanishisms," as Fernande wrote to the poet Guillaume Apollinaire in June 1906. "No tomatoes, or spices, or olives, or anything that can be referred to as *truly Spanish*." There was only authentic Catalan mountain fare. Fernande added, "For example, I could tell you how to make cheese from ewe's milk, or sausage from pork back, or *counill* with aïoli, but it would take too long."

Picasso returned to hunting, one of the pleasures he had learned in Horta. He brought back partridge, thrush, and hare to improve the traditional pot-au-feu or *cocido*, based on beans and sausage,

or a stew called *puchero* served with *pilotas*, large meat balls cooked in bouillon. If these heavy dishes sometimes put off Fernande, who was accustomed to Parisian cooking, they seemed to have the opposite effect on Picasso, giving him tremendous energy for painting. In the mountains, Picasso worked ceaselessly, even between courses while dining with the owner of the inn, Josep Fontdevila, a former blackmarket dealer of questionable character. He sketched unremittingly on his "carnet catalan," the artists' pad he was never without. He carved wood picked up wherever he found it, and painted nonstop.

Picasso mimicked the colors of Horta, such as the large splashes of red earth that illuminated the austere landscape. He seriously applied himself to still life painting, which he had up to now somewhat neglected.

Picasso drinking "à la régalade," in the Spanish tradition, on his birthday, around 1955.

One of his most commonly portrayed subjects was the *porrón*, a pitcher with a long pointed spout meant to be drunk "à la régalade" by holding the *porrón* at arm's length and pouring the wine directly from the spout into one's mouth. Several years later, Picasso continued to delight enthusiastic friends by repeating this gesture of the Catalan shepherds.

Ochre backgrounds, the reds of the peppers and saffron blend together, bottles and *porrón* fade, becoming translucent to contrast the densely opaque crockery, which was another of Picasso's favorite subjects during this period. He delighted in the most humble objects, taking them out of context to paint them in a dreamlike

state while maintaining their form. This is how Picasso lived and worked in Gósol. He was deeply entrenched in the country life, enjoying the "food of the land under the clouds" so much that he likened the woman who brought him bread to a goddess.

Picasso and his friend lived in La Cal Tampanada, one of the only homes in the village equipped with an oven. Women arrived with bread dough wrapped in cloth, and left when the baking was done with large crusty rounds of bread balanced on their heads. Combing through an aroma so thick it appeared to challenge the law of gravity, Picasso painted the human figure and its essential alimentation, bread, so its shape unfolded in a curve suggesting the curve of a woman's lips. He painted in a diffused gold inspired by the earth tones around him and the golden crust of perfectly baked bread, melding in the background both nourishment and the human form.

The oven in Cal Tampanada was used for much more than baking bread. When there was a festival or holiday, the village gathered at Josep's inn. After the usual procession, all were excited to bake the *cuixa de xaï farcida*, stuffed leg of suckling goat, and if the hunt was good on the side of the sierra del Cadi, they roasted wood pigeon larded with bacon and enveloped with prunes and pine nuts; or rack of izard, a type of mountain antelope. The meat was macerated for four to five days in an *escabetx*, or marinade, made by combining fruity olive oil, spices, herbs, seasonings,

Still life of a porrón, 1906, gouache and watercolor on paper. The porrón and the earthenware pitcher are two symbols of his homeland that Picasso held dear.

The Birth of Cubism

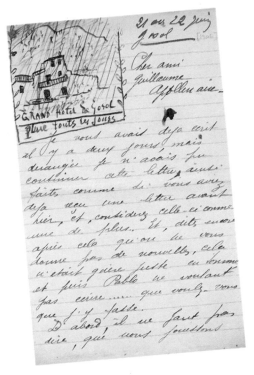

letter from Fernande Olivier to Guillaume Apollinaire at the Grand Hotel in Gósol, June 21 or 22, 1906.

and an aged maderized wine, called *rancio*. Several bottles were passed around the tables as voices grew louder during card playing and the pipe smoke mingled with the aroma of roasting game. The strong winds blew over the sierras, torrents of rain emptied onto the streets and drenched the festival banners, and the atmosphere in the dining room of the inn was transformed from a religious celebration into a pagan feast.

The paintings Picasso made during his stay in Gósol reveal the highlights and colors of this rustic country—gold, pink, fawn. He was also influenced by the welcoming scent of freshly baked bread and roasting leg of lamb, especially appreciated after long hikes in the mountains following the footsteps of shepherds and black market smugglers. But Pablo fled the village when he learned typhoid was in the area. He had a dreaded fear of all illnesses, and took no time to close his suitcases and wave good-bye to his friends before dragging Fernande off with him.

It was three years before Picasso returned to the Catalan mountains in 1909. This time he returned to Horta de Ebro, perhaps because it was there that, ten years before, he had reached somewhat of a turning point in his life. The summer he spent in the mountains in 1898 had brought him in contact with nature for the first time. The experience had been particularly liberating after the intensive study and work in Barcelona and Paris. Now, it was at Horta de Ebro, after the groundwork he laid in Gósol, that Picasso truly came into his own.

"The summer they returned to Spain, they came back to the Spanish countryside: you could almost say it was this countryside [...] that brought about the beginning of cubism," according to one of Picasso's most fervent admirers, the wealthy American intellectual, Gertrude Stein. They met in Paris, where she presented his works from Horta. "It was in these paintings," she added, "that he depicted for the first time the method of constructing the Spanish villages, in which the lines of the houses do not follow the lines of the countryside, but seem to cut into them, and appear to get lost in the very countryside they cut into." During her first stay in the Pyrénées, she admitted to being very impressed "to see how much cubism was a natural outgrowth of Spain."

Yet, even if there is a vast distance between the multifaceted, stacked cubes Picasso painted in 1898 and the actual homes with their balconies, beams, and chimneys, then through his palette he preserved a trace of the past—"the pale yellow and silver with a touch of green, this color is so well known that it is found in most cubist works by Picasso," according to Gertrude Stein. The green of the leaves of the olive trees is a souvenir of Picasso's first stay in Horta; the gold softening into saffron with a streak of powder on grey surfaces combined the beginning of modern painting and the cuisine of Can Tafetans.

Picasso in front of his work titled *L'Aficionado*, painted in 1912.

"*Cubism was a regime, a medication, that healed painting ailing from disorder.*"

Max Jacob

Still life with bread, 1909, oil on canvas.

Barcelona and the Sea

a bove: Printed menu, front and back, for Els Quatre Gats. On the leaflet is the portrait of Père Romeu, 1899–1900.

Opposite: Draft for the menu for Els Quatre Gats, 1899, pen and brown ink.

Els Quatre Gats

There exists another version of the story of the birth of cubism. This one takes place in the city rather than the rustic Catalan mountains, in particular Barcelona and Paris, which played an essential role in the formation and affirmation of Picasso's genius. Cubism, according this story, originated in the heart of the cities, and more precisely, in ambiguously alluring places such as the cafés, bars, brasseries, and cabarets. These were places that challenged morality, where anise and absinthe warmed hearts and conversations, and offered a refuge of boisterous chatter to a complaisant public; to the lonely, the illusion of a club; and for the artists, a never-ending subject of observation and inspiration. "The origin of numerous cubist paintings was based on the transparency of the drinking glasses and the diffraction of the carafes that shattered the light into a thousand facets on the zinc in the cafés," writes Jean-Louis Ferrier.[4]

The first of these legendary places that marked the career of Picasso opened in Barcelona, on June 12, 1897, Els Quatre Gats, The Four Cats. Two years later when Picasso returned, after his stay in Horta, it had become one of the main gathering places for young "modernists" in the Catalan capital. Picasso didn't take long to make it his preferred hangout. The décor and clientele were perfectly matched. The eclectic décor was made up mostly of neo-gothic architecture, and the crowd in the *cerveseris taverna*, or bar, consisted of shoulder-rubbing, decadent dandys; bearded anarchists; and bourgeoisie anxious to glean any new ideas or philosophies.

All shared in the fervor, in a more or less militant manner, for a Catalan Renaissance, a progressive Catalonia. They resolutely turned their backs on Spain, and looked to the two large European metropolises, London and Paris.

The owner of Els Quatre Gats, Pere Romeu, was a gymnastics professor and a master of Chinese shadowgraph. He gave shows in the back room of the tavern to amuse guests and bring in new clients. He wrote the following advertisement for his tavern: Els Quatre Gats is "an inn for those without illusions [...] a museum for those who seek to illuminate their soul [...] a tavern for those in love [...] the essence extracted from a fist full of raisins; a gothic brasserie for those who love the North and an Andalusian patio for those who love the South [...] a place for those in pain to heal, a place for friendship and harmony."[2]

The ambience in the tavern warmed to pitchers of foaming *sengri*, hot wine flavored with cinnamon; or a large glass of *Anís del Mono*, the label of which would be seen several years later in some of Picasso's cubist paintings. Picasso painted and sketched his *tertulia*, his circle of close friends with whom he spent many hours in the tavern, and over which he held an undisputable authority. He expertly played off his ascending reputation and reveled in the competition between his admiring friends over the privilege to be accepted into his confidence and accompany him into the infamous bars and brothels of the Barrio Xino, the Chinese quarter in the port of Barcelona.

The diversity of Picasso's friends wholly reflected the people who frequented Els Quatre Gats. Pallarès, the son of Horta peasants, joined in rejecting the idle rich, such as Carlos Casagemas, who had a penchant for morphine, and promenaded around with his neck constricted in stiff, high collared shirts, flattering himself that he resembled Chopin; or Jaume Sabartès, who was so proud of his authentic Catalan roots that he at first scorned Picasso, before falling under his charm and eventually becoming, thirty-five years later, his secretary and scapegoat.

Right: "We're always ready to drink and eat," proclaims this drawing of the Els Quatre Gats' terrace. Picasso is in the foreground surrounded by his *tertulia*, or social circle, among which Sabartès is standing with his hand behind his back.
Opposite: *Portrait of Jaume Sabartès,* **1900, watercolor and charcoal on paper.**

26

The person Picasso most often dragged along on his excursions to the Barrio Xino was Angel de Soto, who was "always amusing, no matter what,"[6] as described by Picasso. De Soto also impressed Picasso with his melancholy elegance, to the point that Picasso carefully copied de Soto's gestures, such as posing with studied casualness with a hand in his pocket.

In addition to the artists with little real talent who dabbled at painting, were those who were already recognized: Ramón Casas, who portrayed himself and Pere Romeu riding a tandem bicycle in a large painted poster that covered the wall of the large room of the tavern; and Joaquím Mir, a landscape artist who used strong colors, contrary to Spanish tradition. Mir was one of Picasso's favorite caricature models.

*P*ortrait of Carlos Casagemas,
1899–1900, oil on canvas.

Tongue in cheek, Picasso sketched Els Quatre Gats regulars: Casagemas in his stiff, high collar; Mir, always with an eye on women's legs; and Pere Romeu, forever wearing his cordoba hat. Romeu, the owner, was very much aware of Picasso's talent, and asked him to illustrate the menus and leaflets for the tavern. For this, Picasso easily adapted the eclectic surroundings of the tavern to Catalonia's modern art. On the terrace of Els Quatre Gats, he posed people dressed in the fitted coats and crinoline skirts of the 1830s in front of the "gothic" entrance designed by Puig i Cadafalch, one of the most talented young modernist architects, to purposely exaggerate the anachronism. Picasso borrowed this style, using strong, thick black lines to outline shapes, from the English art nouveau, in particular Aubrey Beardsley and Kate Greenaway. This colored stylization strongly contrasted to the noisy, smoky reality inside the tavern, and the heavy regional cuisine. Imagine a young debonair with a carnation in his lapel, hand on a hip, diving into a plate of Catalan tripe generously flavored with garlic, or one of the many specialties based on *baccalà,* salted codfish.

This modest fish had the effect of stimulating the inventive spirit of the Catalonian. One of the popular dishes in Barcelona was codfish stuffed with robustly flavored ham and peppers; near the village of Bagés, codfish was cut into cubes, covered with raisins, and coated with *picada,* a boldly flavored white wine sauce blended with almonds, cinnamon stick, garlic, and hot red pepper; the Montserrat monks prepared a succulent brandade of salted cod; and everywhere it was prepared in classic Catalan style, with *samfaïna,* a coulis of tomato, onion, eggplant, and peppers, ingredients every household had on hand to prepare their own personalized version. There were endless passionate disputes over the "best" preparation. The local gastronomic chronicler, Josep Pla,[7] was known to say "*samfaãna* improves all dishes and endows fundamental optimism."

Picasso alongside Mateu de Soto, Angel de Soto's brother and art critic at the *El Liberal*,
and Carlos Casagemas, on the terrace of 3 Merce Street in Barcelona, 1900.

However, in regard to the culinary arts, the guests at Els Quatre Gats were willing to loosen up on their uncompromising Catalonianism. They tolerated Basque-style cod on the menu, regardless of its origin; as well as the Estrémaduran ham soup, and of course, the *gazpacho*, which they could quickly recognize as Andalousian.

Sundays at the Home of Casagemas

Sundays, the same group from the tavern gathered at Carlos Casagemas's house in Nou de la Rambla square. His parents allotted him a section of their spacious apartment, which he transformed into an atelier, and where he received

the rowdy Bohemian *decadentes* and *anarquistas*. Casagemas would spout a few romantic poems of his own, or launch into a stream of apologies regarding his drug and alcohol abuse, which he defended as being the only way to excite the creative faculties, to which Picasso virulently disagreed.

The ritual drink served on these Sunday gatherings was a specially prepared coffee. Cognac, sugar, clove, and cinnamon were heated in a copper pot on a wood-burning stove, and flambéed amidst the enthusiastic exclamations of the group. Strong, steaming hot coffee was added to the flaming mixture, and it was served immediately. Discussions calmed down during this ceremony,

only to take on more vigor once the cups were emptied. Some, warmed and loosened up after drinking, went so far as to sing the prohibited Catalonian hymns.

It was in this spirited atmosphere that Picasso was introduced to one of the only modern

painters he sincerely admired at the time, Isidro Nonell. Contrary to Casagemas or Sabartès, Nonell was raised in very modest surroundings. His father sold pasta in a poor section of Barcelona. Nonell himself quickly turned against the academic paintings touted as "art for art's sake." He preferred to hang out with gypsies and others excluded by society such as the "cretins of Bohí," outcasts who took refuge in the outskirts of Catalonia. His drawings of these people were published in a newspaper and created quite a sensation. Picasso was unable to remain indifferent to this powerful work, which showed a complete break from the orderly aesthetics of the time.

After gaining renown, Nonell divided his time between Barcelona and Paris. In Paris, he rented an atelier which he warmly offered to his friends, and where Picasso stayed during his first trip to Paris. Still, Picasso had to make a living. He sold several caricatures and *dibujos fritos*, or fried sketches, to customers at Els Quatre Gats. Nonell had become a specialist of this technique and handed on his "recipe" to Picasso: heat a pan with oil, throw in the sketch, and cook it while constantly shaking the pan; the sketch will take on an attractive sepia tint. As soon as the edges start to roll up, take the sketch out of the pan. The paper will have taken on the patina of old parchment.

These sketches were sold to antiques lovers, after a beguiling discussion as to the rarity of the work.

Several years later, between 1936 and 1938, Picasso thought back to these fried sketches made on Sunday afternoons at Casagemas's home and referred to them in his *Writings:* "the sketches were dripping with oil," followed by a series of metaphors that joined cooking and painting. A painting appeared to be "drowning in a silver platter of soup," the color was "picked-up in a potato omelette," the vegetables were "painted in their natural colors complete with fragrance, spirit, and style." The "colors of the mustard pots were put into a paint tube" as he compared painting to cooking; holding a palette in the fashion of a frying pan, elaborating recipes, mixing ingredients, simmering an idea, and finally serving a *chef-d'oeuvre* to admiring guests.

The fake "old" sketches that Nonell introduced to Picasso no doubt fired his imagination, in which cooking, food, and creativity merged. Picasso "devoured" a particular view of the world, which he digested, then restored, transformed into colored paint on his canvas. The tan hues of the *dibujos fritos* evoked the "black manner" of the *Caprices* of Goya, occupying an important place in Picasso's unconscious, to reappear in 1937, when the civil war tore Spain apart, profoundly affecting Picasso's life and art. Nineteen thirty-seven was the year of Picasso's *Guernica*, and his poem *The Dream and Lie of Franco*, in which he writes:

"The flag writhes about as we fry it in the black sauce made from spilling ink." Here, suffering and mourning transform two allusions to a Spain now lost—the Sundays with Nonell at Casagemas's home, and the days of *marisquerias* on the beaches between Stiges and Cadaqués, where they dined on octopus and cuttlefish cooked in ink.

The Mediterranean

Picasso's Catalonia was not restricted to the capital and the mountain villages. In Barcelona, the avenues end at the sea, two steps from the Barrio Xino where the taverns were frequented by sailors, where outbursts were heard in all languages over cheating at cards, women, or nothing at all. Here, the wine is coarse, the liquor dubious and most likely watered down, but the fried fish sprinkled with lemon juice is often exquisite. Picasso reveled in these dives at least as much as at the more fashionable Els Quatre Gats. The aroma of frying fish drifted into narrow streets filled with the sounds of snapping fingers, guitar melodies, laughter, all melding together to sometimes include the din of a distant brawl and the shattering of glass.

The Mediterranean is impregnated by the atmosphere of the city, the sun blankets the coast that Pablo explored with his friend, Ramón Pichot. Pichot was ten years Pablo's senior, and came from a wealthy family. His apartment on Montcada Street was a meeting place for artists. All members of the Pichot family were involved in the arts. Maria, one of his sisters, often sang at Els Quatre

above: Fernande Olivier, Picasso, and writer Ramón Reventos, 1906, in Reventos's home, a gathering place for all the Barcelona artists, and, according to Picasso, "where it all began."
Opposite: Postcard sent from Picasso to Apollinaire in Cadaquès, July 5, 1910.

Picasso was content to immortalize the clientele of Els Quatre Gats, "a group of unknown and mostly poorly dressed," as Sabartès wrote, not without malevolence. But in portraying this collection of Bohemian, penniless, unsuccessful dreamers, the young artist displayed his stupendous virtuosity. He gave himself the luxury of parodying the poses of Casas's models without turning them into caricatures. Manuel Pallarès and Angel de Soto, along with the other artists faithful to Picasso's group, were portrayed with a rare intensity. He worked in charcoal offset by watercolor to give his portraits an incomplete, barely sketched quality to correspond to his subjects, giving the work a somewhat coarse style. To accentuate the rich brown tones, Picasso would sometimes spill the last of his coffee into the middle of his watercolors.

Picasso's first exhibition opened February 1, 1900. Due to a lack of funds, the art works were not framed, but nailed directly to the walls of the large room in Els Quatre Gats. The regulars who came to view the work were, according to Sabartès, "the most assiduous. Because we can all find more or less the time to go there [...] to drink a coffee and chat with friends." The "art-going" public ignored the exhibition, discouraged by the critics who barely warmed to the work, or panned it outright.

But the new century was to prove very favorable for Picasso. Despite less than enthusiastic reviews, he sold several portraits, which enabled him to move into an *orbrador*, or atelier, which he shared with Casagemas on the top floor of a dilapidated building on the narrow street, Sant Joan. The artists decorated this uncomfortable attic according to their imagination. Picasso painted the walls with a luxurious bed, an open safe stuffed with fantastic riches, and a comely, full-figured chambermaid. He completed the *trompe-l'oeil* with sumptuous bouquets of flowers and pyramids of skillfully arranged fruits. On the partitions of the atelier he painted a horn of plenty filled with a magnificent assortment of fruits such as figs and grapes, oranges, lemons, melons, and cherries.

This Ali Baba cavern quickly became too confining for the two painters. In spite of the panorama of the Barcelona roofs, they dreamed of other horizons. They became seriously absorbed in planning a venture to Paris. To gather the necessary funds was not a simple task—they were obliged to convince their reticent families to lend them money. They alerted friends who owned a *pied-à-terre* in Paris. They ordered black velvet suits with fully cut jackets, and pants that were tightly wrapped around their ankles. In this way they would appear fashionable among the Parisian artists, who were known for their casual elegance, at least according to popular opinion in Barcelona.

A few days before his nineteenth birthday, in October 1900, Picasso boarded the train to Paris accompanied by Casagemas.

*P*icasso and Sebastian Junyer on the way to Paris, 1904, one of the five drawings in ink and color pencil immortalizing Picasso's forth trip to Paris handwritten: "In a third class car they are heading towards the frontier."

Appetizers
Garlic rubbed bread with tomatoes
Gazpacho
Garlic soup with tomato and Estrémaduran ham
Cadaquès mussel brochettes
Sardines escabéche

Main Courses
Catalan tripes
Saffron rice
Horta Cocido
Roasted rack of Izard
Garlic rabbit
Aïoli
Rice cooked in broth
Basquc-style codfish
Gambas sautéed in garlic
Oven roasted vegetables
Zarzuela
Squid casserole
Montserrat monk's salted codfish

Desserts
Els Quatre Gats Sengri
Honey and aniseed fritters

Garlic Rubbed Bread
with Tomato

FOUR SERVINGS

3 round tomatoes	6 tbsp extra virgin olive oil
2 garlic cloves	salt and pepper, to taste
4 slices country bread, ¾-inch thick	6 arugula leaves

✴ Preheat the oven to 350°F(180°C). Wash and dry the tomatoes. Slice two of the tomatoes into ¼-inch slices; leave one whole and set it aside. Peel the garlic cloves. Toast the sliced bread in the oven on both sides for 6 minutes, or until golden.

✴ Allow the toasts to cool. Rub one side of each toast with a peeled garlic clove, then rub with the whole tomato. Sprinkle the toasts with half the oil and cover with the tomato slices, overlapping. Season with salt and pepper. Sprinkle with the remaining olive oil. Tear the arugula leaves and evenly distribute them over the toasts. The toasts can be cut in halves or thirds. Serve immediately.

Gazpacho

FOUR SERVINGS

1 large onion	5 tbsp extra virgin olive oil
2 garlic cloves	4 tbsp xérès or red wine vinegar
5 tomatoes	1 pinch cayenne pepper
1 medium cucumber	salt and freshly ground pepper, to taste
1 green pepper	3 slices day-old white bread
4¼ cups water	

✴ Peel and chop the onion and set aside in a bowl. Peel and chop the garlic and place it in the bowl of a food processor. Peel the tomato, remove and discard the seeds. Cut the tomato and the cucumber into small cubes. Reserve 2 tablespoons of each for garnish and place the rest in the bowl with the onion. Cut the green pepper in half, and remove and discard the seeds and white pith. Cut the pepper into cubes. Reserve one tablespoon and place the remainder in the bowl. Cut the bread into small cubes. Reserve 3 tablespoons for the garnish and place the remainder in the food processor. Add the oil, vinegar, cayenne pepper, salt and black pepper to the food processor. Process for 2 minutes. Add the contents of the bowl. Process for an additional 5 minutes, gradually pouring in the water.

✴ Pour the purée through a strainer and into a soup tureen. Taste and add salt and pepper as needed. Refrigerate for 3 hours. Serve the gazpacho well chilled, garnished with the cubed bread and vegetables.

Garlic soup with tomato and Estrémaduran ham

10 garlic cloves	2 pinches powdered hot pepper
scant ½ cup olive oil	4 thyme branches
4 tomatoes	1 Estrémaduran, or smoked ham bone
4¼ cups water	croutons rubbed with garlic, as needed
salt and pepper to taste	

✳ Peel the garlic cloves and cut them in quarters, removing and discarding the central germ. Heat the oil in a heavy-bottomed saucepan over low heat. Add the garlic and cook for 2 minutes to bring out the flavor without browning, stirring constantly. Cut the tomatoes in quarters and add them to the saucepan. Cook gently for 10 minutes. Pour in the water. Season to taste with salt and pepper. Add the powdered hot pepper, thyme, and ham bone. Cover and simmer for 2 hours. Remove the ham bone and strain the soup. Taste and add salt and pepper if needed. Serve in a soup tureen, preferably earthenware. Serve with toasted or fried croutons rubbed with garlic.

Cadaquès Mussel Brochettes

FOUR SERVINGS

2 garlic cloves	2 thick bacon slices
3 tablespoons olive oil	8 bay leaves
salt and pepper to taste	saffron rice (recipe page 42)
generous 2 lbs large mussels	

✳ Preheat the oven to 475°F(240°C) with a baking sheet inside. Peel the garlic cloves, place them in a bowl, sprinkle with olive oil, and crush them. Season with salt and pepper. Set aside to marinate. Meanwhile, wash the mussels in cold water, remove any sand, and pull off the beards. Spread the cleaned mussels on the hot baking sheet. Cook them in the oven for approximately 6 minutes or until they open. Take them out of the oven and set them aside to cool. Remove them from their shells, reserving any juices. To blanch the bacon, cut the strips into ¼ in pieces.° Bring a small saucepan of water to a boil and plunge the bacon in the boiling water. Cook for 30 minutes, then drain and set aside to cool.
✳ On each of four skewers, arrange the following: one bay leaf folded in half, then 4 mussels alternated with 4 bacon pieces, then a second folded bay leaf. Using a brush, dab the brochettes with the garlic marinated olive oil. Cook the brochettes on a hot grill for 10 minutes, turning them around halfway through cooking. Serve hot with saffron rice.
° If the bacon is not very salty, the blanching can be omitted

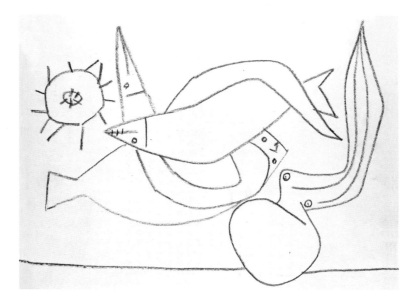

ƒ ish, 1946, pencil on paper.

Sardines escabèche

FOUR SERVINGS

generous 2 lbs fresh sardines	*2 bay leaves*
¾ cup olive oil	*2 pinches thyme*
2 garlic cloves	*1 cup white wine vinegar*
2 onions	*1 cup rancio (white maderized wine)*
2 carrots	*1 tsp tomato paste*
½ red chili pepper	*salt and pepper to taste*

✳ Bone and cut the heads off the sardines. Heat 5 tablespoons of the oil in a sauté pan, over high heat. Add the sardines and cook for 3 minutes on each side until golden brown. Drain them on paper towels and set them aside to cool. Peel the garlic cloves, onions, and carrots. Cut the onions into thin slices, and grate the carrots. Chop the red chili pepper. Finely chop the bay leaves. Heat the remaining oil in a saucepan and gently cook the onions until tender. When the onions are translucent, add the carrots, vinegar, wine, garlic, red chili pepper, bay leaves, thyme, and tomato paste. Season with salt and pepper to taste. Cook for 20 minutes, stirring gently. Taste to verify the seasonings.

✳ Pour one-third of the escabèche onto a platter. Arrange half of the sardines on top. Cover with a second third of the escabèche. Arrange the remaining sardines on top. Cover with the final third of the escabèche. Cover and place in the refrigerator to marinate for 3 days before serving.

Catalan Tripes

FOUR SERVINGS

Court-bouillon:	*3 onions*
2 bay leaves	*6 garlic cloves*
1 rosemary branch	*2 tomatoes*
1 celery rib	*2 medium eggplants*
3 thyme branches	*1 red pepper*
1 leek	*8 tbsp olive oil*
2 carrots	*generous 1½ lbs tripe, blanched*
1 onion, stuck with a clove	*1 pinch thyme*
1 cup dry white wine	*salt and pepper to taste*
1 tbsp coarse salt	*saffron rice (recipe below)*
8½ cups water	

✳ To prepare the court-bouillon, place the ingredients listed in the left column for the court-bouillon in the water. Bring to a boil. Add the tripe and simmer for 3 hours. Remove the tripe, drain, and reserve the tripe and court-bouillon separately.

✳ Peel and chop the onion and garlic. Peel and seed the tomatoes and cut into cubes. Rinse the eggplants and cut into large cubes. Rinse the red pepper, remove the seeds and pith, and cut into large cubes.

✳ Heat the oil in a deep pan or casserole. Brown the well-drained tripe on all sides. Remove the tripe from the pan and set aside on a plate. Place the onions and garlic in the pan and cook over low heat. When they are translucent, add the tomatoes, red pepper, eggplant, and thyme. Cook for 10 minutes. Add the tripe. Season to taste with salt and pepper. Cover and cook slowly for 1 hour at a light simmer. Occasionally add some court-bouillon during the cooking to keep the ingredients moist. Serve with saffron rice.

Saffron Rice

FOUR SERVINGS

2 pinches saffron	*3½ cups water*
¼ cup water	*sea salt to taste*
1½ cups white rice	

✳ Bring the ¼ cup water to a boil. Add the saffron and set aside to infuse for 20 minutes. Rinse the rice with cold water until the water runs off clear. Bring the 3 ½ cups water to a boil in a large saucepan. Add the salt and infused water. Sprinkle in the rice. Cover and cook over low heat for approximately 15 minutes, or until all the water is absorbed.

Horta Cocido

A *COCIDO* IS A SPANISH STEW; THIS ONE COMES FROM THE HORTA REGION.
FOUR SERVINGS

9 oz dried chickpeas	3.5 oz chorizo (optional)
1 salted pig's foot	5 oz wide noodles
1 ham hock or pork shin	salt and pepper to taste
generous 1 lb beef shank	For the pilotas:
9 oz bacon, not smoked	3.5 oz pork filet, ground
1 small chicken or game bird	7 oz sausage meat
1 onion, stuck with 2 cloves	2 tablespoons white bread crumbs
2 bay leaves	2 eggs
2 carrots	2 garlic cloves
2 turnips	2 tablespoons chopped parsley
6 potatoes	2 pinches ground cinnamon
1 green cabbage	salt and pepper to taste
9 oz blood sausage	3 tbsp flour

✳ Soak the chickpeas (Castile, if available) covered with water in a bowl for 12 hours. Draw the salt out of the pig's foot and ham hock by covering with cold water and soaking for 12 hours.

✳ Place the beef shank, bacon, chicken or game bird, soaked pig's foot, and ham hock in a large stockpot. Completely cover with cold water. Bring to a boil and constantly skim off any froth or scum that rises to the surface. When the bouillon is clear, add the onion and bay leaves. Tie the chick peas in cheese cloth and place them in the casserole; this way they can be easily taken out when cooked. Add the salt, but not the pepper, and simmer over low heat for 2 hours.

✳ Meanwhile, prepare the *pilotas:* in a bowl, combine the ground pork filet, sausage meat, bread crumbs, eggs, chopped garlic, parsley, and cinnamon. Season with salt and pepper. Combine the mixture until well blended. Shape into 4 balls and roll them in the flour. Set the meat balls aside on a plate.

✳ Prepare the vegetables. Peel the carrots, turnips, and potatoes. After the stew has cooked for 2 hours, add vegetables, blood sausage, sliced chorizo, and the *pilotas*. Continue cooking for 40 minutes.

✳ After 40 minutes, remove 4 cups of bouillon (cooking liquid from the stew) and use it to cook the noodles. When the noodles are cooked, pour them and the bouillon into a soup tureen. Cut the meat into serving-sized pieces and present them, moistened with bouillon, in a shallow bowl. Place the vegetables on a separate plate and serve all three items at the same time.

Rack of Izard

**IZARD IS A SMALL MOUNTAIN ANTELOPE; VENISON MAKES A GOOD SUBSTITUTE.
FOUR SERVINGS**

MARINADE:	*SAUCE:*
1 bottle (12.5 fl oz) rancio	*4 shallots*
(maderized white wine, or muscat)	*2 tomatoes or 1.5 oz (50 g) dried*
½ cup red wine vinegar	*tomatoes*
8 tbsp olive oil	*14 oz mushrooms*
2 thyme branches	*7 oz bacon, cut in small cubes*
2 bay leaves	*3 tbsp olive oil*
1 rack of izard or venison	*2 tbsp white wine*
7 oz fatback, thinly sliced	*¾ cup chicken stock*
	salt and pepper to taste
	2 tsp chopped watercress or flat leaf
	parsley
	rice cooked in broth (recipe page 48)

✳ Combine the ingredients listed for the marinade. Add the rack of izard or venison and marinate for 3–5 days depending on the size and age of the meat. Turn the meat around once a day so all sides marinate. Before cooking, drain the meat well. Strain and reserve the marinade. Lard the rack by tying the fatback around the meat with butcher twine. Dab the larded rack with the olive oil. Roast the rack in an oven preheated to 500°F(250°C). Calculate 11–12 minutes per pound of meat. Baste the meat occasionally throughout roasting.

✳ Meanwhile, prepare the sauce. Peel and finely chop the shallots. Plunge the tomatoes in boiling water for 3 seconds, take them out, peel off the skin and seed them. Roughly chop the peeled, seeded tomatoes. Roughly chop the mushrooms. Cut the bacon into small cubes or strips. Heat the oil in a saucepan and cook the shallots over a low heat until translucent. Add the bacon, mushrooms, and tomato. Moisten with the wine and stock. Lightly season with salt and pepper. Simmer, covered, on low heat for 20 minutes. Add the chopped watercress or parsley at the end of cooking.

✳ Pour the sauce into a sauce boat and serve it with the rack along with rice cooked in broth.

Garlic rabbit

FOUR SERVINGS

2 onions	*1 cup dry white wine (penedés or alella)*
6 tbsp olive oil	*1 rosemary branch*
1 rabbit, cut in portions	*1 thyme branch*
salt and pepper to taste	*6 garlic cloves, unpeeled*
1 tbsp moderate red pepper (capsicum)	*aïoli (recipe below)*

✳ Preheat the oven to 350°F(180°C). Peel and slice the onions. Cook them in a deep oven-proof casserole with the oil until tender and translucent. Add the rabbit and brown on all sides. This step can be done with a few pieces at a time depending on the size of the pan, so each piece cooks flat. After all pieces are browned, place them all in the pan. Season with salt, freshly milled pepper, and red pepper. Add the wine, herbs, and garlic with the skin. Cover and bake in the oven for 40 minutes. Serve with the aïoli.

Aïoli

6 garlic cloves	*1 egg yolk*
salt and pepper to taste	*1 cup olive oil*
juice of ¼ lemon	

✳ Peel the garlic. Place the cloves in a mortar and crush them with a pestle to obtain a smooth paste. Season with salt and freshly milled pepper. Add the lemon juice and egg yolk. Gradually whisk in the olive oil, pouring slowly, as for a mayonnaise, until the mixture thickens. Test for seasoning, adding salt and pepper if needed.

G arlic rabbit and aïoli (follow page).

recipes

Zarzuela

SIX SERVINGS

Fish Stock (Fumet):	2 thick slices Serrano ham
2 fish heads	generous 2 lbs mussels
1 onion	generous 1 lb cockles
1 cup dry white wine	3 rock lobsters or standard lobsters
2 bay leaves	14 oz squid
3 thyme branches	½ cup olive oil
3 parsley sprigs	5 parsley sprigs
1 leek	12 large shrimp or crawfish
1 celery rib	generous 1 lb monkfish, cut into 6 pieces
coarse sea salt to taste	3 pinches powdered saffron
3 onions	1 cup cognac
6 garlic cloves	salt and pepper to taste
1 green pepper	18 toasted bread slices, rubbed with
½ hot red pepper	garlic

✳ Prepare the fish stock. In a large saucepan put the fish heads, peeled onion, white wine, and bouquet garni made by tying the bay leaves, thyme, parsley, leek greens, and celery rib together with butcher twine. Cover with water. Add salt to taste. Bring to a boil and simmer gently for 1 hour.

✳ Meanwhile, peel and finely chop the onions and garlic. Plunge the tomatoes in boiling water for 3 seconds. Peel and seed them, then chop them finely. Remove the pith and seeds of the green pepper and hot red pepper, then slice them lengthwise. Cut the ham into strips. Wash, scrub, and debeard the mussels. Scrub the cockles. Drain the mollusks well. Separate the heads and claws of the lobster and cut the tails in half, lengthwise to extract the flesh. The claws can be added to the stock and cooked for the last 20 minutes to add flavor. Slice the squid in rings.

✳ In a large stock pot, heat 3 tablespoons olive oil and cook the onions and garlic over low heat. When the onion is translucent and tender, add the chopped tomatoes and chopped parsley. Cook for 10 minutes, then set aside.

✳ In a large, heavy-bottomed skillet (such as a cast-iron skillet), heat 3 tablespoons olive oil and quickly sear the lobster tails. Remove them with a metal spatula and place them in the stock pot. One at a time, sear the shrimp, squid, monkfish, ham, and green pepper. After each item is cooked, place it in the pot. Add oil as needed to sear the ingredients. Add 3 cups strained stock to the pot, along with the hot pepper, saffron, and cognac. Season with salt and freshly milled pepper to taste. Stir gently. Cover and simmer for 20 minutes. In a separate pot, steam the mussels over high heat just until they open. Add them along with their cooking juices to the stock pot. Repeat with the cockles. Cook for 5 minutes. Place 3 slices of the garlic-rubbed toasts on each plate and serve the soup over them.

recipes

Squid Casserole

FOUR SERVINGS

SAUCE	STUFFING
1 lb + 10.5 oz tomatoes	*1 onion*
2 onions	*4 garlic cloves*
5 garlic cloves	*5 parsley sprigs*
6 parsley sprigs	*2 tbsp bread crumbs or day-old bread*
2 thyme branches	*9 oz air-cured ham*
1 bay leaf	*3.5 oz almond powder*
3 parsley sprigs	*2 pinches powdered hot pepper*
1 celery rib	*4 medium or 8 small squid*
salt and pepper to taste	*1 cup cognac*
6 tbsp olive oil	*scant ¾ cup dry white wine*

✳ Prepare the sauce. Peel and seed the tomatoes, and cut them in eighths. Peel and chop the onions. Peel and smash the garlic. Chop the 6 sprigs of parsley. Heat 3 tablespoons olive oil in a saucepan. Cook the onions and garlic until translucent and tender. Add the tomatoes, and a bouquet garni, made by tying the thyme, bay leaf, parsley, and celery together with butcher twine. Season with salt and pepper to taste. Moisten with a little water and cook over low heat for 15–20 minutes. Add water during cooking if the tomatoes do not release much juice as the mixture should be moist.

✳ Meanwhile, prepare the stuffing. Peel and finely chop the onion and garlic. Chop the parsley. Grind the bread into breadcrumbs. Cut the ham into small cubes. Place all the ingredients except for the onions in a bowl. Add the almond powder and powdered hot pepper. Set aside.

✳ Clean and eviscerate the squids, being careful not to tear the bodies. Chop the tentacles and other edible parts taken from the interior, leaving the bodies whole. Heat a small amount of olive oil and cook the reserved onions. Add the chopped squid and cook over high heat until browned. Add the mixture to the bowl with the stuffing. Season with salt and pepper and blend well. Fill the squid bodies two-thirds full with the stuffing. Seal the openings with toothpicks.

✳ Heat the remaining olive oil in a heavy bottomed saucepan. Brown the stuffed squid on all sides. Flambé with the cognac and add the wine. Bring to a boil, then add the tomato sauce and saffron. Simmer, covered, over low heat for 45 minutes. Serve in individual earthenware crocks.

Montserrat Monks' Salted Codfish

FOUR SERVINGS

1 lb + 10.5 oz salted codfish	*1 oz day-old bread or breadcrumbs*
14 oz potatoes	*1 tbsp + 2 tsp butter*
1 onion	*salt to taste*
6 garlic cloves	*croutons rubbed with garlic as needed*
¾ cup olive oil	

✳ Soak the codfish in cold water for 12 hours, changing the water several times during this period. Rinse the codfish after soaking. Place it in a saucepan. Completely cover with cold water. Bring to a boil. Lower the heat and simmer for 15 minutes. The codfish should flake easily with a fork when done. Drain the fish, remove the skin and bones, and pull the flesh apart. Cook the potatoes with their skin in a pot of salted water. When tender, drain, peel, and cut into cubes. Peel and chop the onions and garlic.

✳ In a saucepan, heat 2 tablespoons olive oil and cook the onion until tender. Add the garlic and cook gently without browning. Add the potatoes and the flaked codfish; smash the mixture into a purée. In a separate pot, bring the milk to a boil. Slowly add the remaining olive oil and boiling hot milk to the purée, stirring constantly. Spread the mixture in a well oiled oven-proof dish. Grind the bread into breadcrumbs and sprinkle them on the purée. Scatter small cubes of butter on top. Brown in a hot oven at 500°F(250°C) for 10 minutes. Serve with croutons rubbed with garlic.

Els Quatre Gats Sengri

MAKES EIGHT GLASSES

one bottle red wine	*4 tbsp acacia honey*
1 cinnamon stick	*2 tbsp cognac*
zest of 3 organic oranges	*1 cup boiling water*
3 cloves	

✳ Pour the wine into a saucepan and add the cinnamon stick. Heat on high heat. As soon as the wine comes to a boil, add the orange zest and cloves. Bring back to a boil. Add the honey, cognac, and water. Serve hot in thick, heat-proof glasses.

Honey and aniseed fritters

MAKES 12 TO 15 FRITTERS

2 eggs, separated	*1 tsp eau-de-vie (brandy)*
scant 1 cup flour	*1 tbsp olive oil*
½ tbsp fresh lemon juice	*oil for deep frying*
1 pinch salt	*chestnut honey*
	aniseed to taste

✳ Separate the eggs. Lightly oil the work surface. Place the flour in a mound over the oiled surface. Make in indentation in the center of the flour, and fill with the egg yolks, oil, lemon juice, salt, and eau-de-vie. Gradually work the flour into the center, blending all ingredients. Add water as needed if the mixture is dry. When the ingredients are well blended, place the batter in a bowl covered with plastic wrap, and set aside in a warm area for 2 hours.

✳ Whip the egg whites to medium peaks and fold them into the rested batter. Heat the deep-frying oil to 340°F(170°C). Roll out the dough ¼ inch thick. Cut the sheet of dough into 12 squares and fold each square over once or twice. Carefully place the dough in the hot oil and cook until golden brown on all sides. Remove the fritters from the oil and drain them on paper towels.

✳ Drizzle honey on the fritters and sprinkle with aniseed. Serve hot.

were eating that day, which made up nearly every meal at this time, was almost as appetizing as the Catalan sobresadas that hung in butcher shops in Barcelona. But as soon as a fork was impatiently planted through the skin of the sausage, there was an explosion of rancid grease. The delicious looking sausages, it turned out, were merely filled with gas and fat. The two friends, each more hungry than the other, saw the possibility of a good meal vanish into thin air.

Years later, Picasso never missed an opportunity to tell this story when talking about his early years in Paris. The location and details might vary according to his whim but the sausage always ended up exploding. This misadventure was symbolic of the tainted food that replaced the flavorful Barcelona specialties Picasso was used to.

Bohemia

"The angry cow"

Picasso took four years to fully establish himself in Paris. Between October 1900 and April 1904 he made three trips to Paris, the city of lights, where his hopes were often shattered. Yet, he returned. He believed without doubt that no other place could offer him such freedom. "If Cézanne had worked in Spain," he declared one day, "they would have burned him alive."[1] Casagemas, who accompanied Picasso on his first trip to Paris wrote to a friend who had remained in Barcelona, "Here, there is a place for everyone." Far from his family, far from the prejudgments in Madrid and the provincial Catalan thinking, Picasso was finally able to show what he was capable of.

He was able to prove himself in the autumn of 1900. He set himself up in Nonell's atelier on Gabrielle street in the Montmartre quarter of Paris. There he took on the same subjects that had made Renoir, Degas, and Toulouse-Lautrec famous. *Chanteuse de la café-concert, La Danseuse bleue, Le Moulin de la Galette . . .* these were some of Picasso's first works in Paris, made in defiance of his illustrious elders. In these designs, the lines cut almost cruelly into the violently con-

trasting darkness. The young Spanish painter, now nineteen years old, showed that he was not envious of the artists who preceded him in the fashionable spots of "gay Paris." These legendary places were, according to Casagemas, in full decline: "Here, all is wrapped up in fanfare, gaudy imitation, [. . .] papier-mâché stuffed with sawdust [. . .]. The Moulin de la Galette has lost all its character and entrance to the *idem* Rouge costs three francs, and on some days five." On the other hand, the boulevard de Clichy offered a variety of offbeat places, such as Les 4 z'Arts, Le Néant, and L'Enfer, where the well-known cabaret singer Aristide Bruant, with his hard look and red scarf, became the emblem of Montmartrian nights.

The "Catalan gang" from then on included in its ranks Pallarés, who came from Horta, and Pichot, who established himself on the other side of Montmartre in the small, pink *Maison*. They lived as much outside in the cafés and brasseries as in the uncomfortable ateliers and hotel rooms where it was impossible to cook. After days of fasting they would find themselves in front of one of the beef ragoûts that dethroned the *puchero* and *cocido*—mutton stew. "Nothing makes a better ragoût than mutton, but I much prefer a miroton or a good bourguignon," proclaimed Picasso in "Desire

*P*icasso and *Junyer arrive in Paris*, 1904, drawing in ink and colored pencils (see page 35)
with the caption: "At nine o'clock in the morning we have finally arrived in Paris."

Caught by the Tail," the play he wrote in 1941. During the lean days there was always a friend who would find a few sous in his pocket, which started the ritual that was written down by the painter many years later, "We would buy cheese and bread and eat seated on a bench." At place du Tertre or place Ravignan they did not savor the "young goat cheeses wrapped in milk paper with grape seeds," but rather a soft, oozing Brie or ripe,

creamy Camembert. These cheeses were one of the enthusiastic discoveries Picasso made in Paris.

When Picasso returned to Barcelona after a difficult winter in 1902–1903, he wrote to Max Jacob to invite him to come to Spain for the summer. He scribbled a few words between two drawings of the roofs that he saw looking down from his atelier: "My dear old Max, I think of the room on boulevard Voltaire, the omelettes, beans, brie cheese, and french fries, but I am also thinking of the days of poverty, and I become very sad when I remember, with disgust, the Spaniards on the rue de Seine . . ."

The culinary specialties of the Spaniards on the rue de Seine seemed as tainted to Picasso as the outlandish spectacles evoked by Casagemas: "Some nights we go to cafés, concerts, or theaters. . . . Sometimes they think they are doing Spanish dances, and yesterday one of them let go with a fart of 'Olé olé! Caramba caramba!' that left us cold and made us doubt our origins." The effervescence of the nights, the packed clubs, the intoxicated crowds, the trays full of beer glasses, the laughter coming from lipstick covered lips, was merely a display, Picasso knew, to hide their sad-

ness. Paris was not just one big party. When the mimes and acrobats finished their acts, they sat still in their many-colored costumes at a table in front of a glass of absinthe, the "luminous poison"[2] that brilliantly shined with phosphorus reflections and drove one into an endless dazed stupor—the *Pierreuses au bar* with weighed down, hunched over, naked shoulders. Blue engulfed everything. The world was ravaged by this color, which was like the bitter taste of misery and despair. The beginning of Picasso's Blue Period coincided with one of the most difficult events in his life—Carlos Casagemas's suicide. In addition to grief over losing his friend, Picasso suffered the inconsolable remorse that he had not been nearby at the time.

above and opposite: *Alleluia*, illustrated letter to Miguel Utrillo,
June 1901, ink and colored pencil on paper.
Following pages: The Bateau-Lavoir, at place Emile-Goudeau in Paris.

After several months in Paris, Picasso and Casagemas decided to return to Spain. They went to Málaga, where their manners and shabby dress were the talk of the town. Picasso postponed his return to France, leaving his friend to go alone. It was there that Casagemas fell in love with Germaine, a young and beautiful woman who called herself a model and led a happy life among the artists in Montmartre. On February 17, 1901, after having been rejected by her, Casagemas killed himself. "It was while thinking that Casagemas was dead that I started to paint in blue," Picasso

would confirm much later to one of his biographers, Pierre Daix.

In autumn 1901 Picasso painted the portrait *The Poet Sabartès*, of his friend seated at a café table. After much hesitation Sabartès had decided to make the trip to Paris. "The mania to go to Paris ravaged us," as he wrote in *Picasso, Portraits and Souvenirs*, "I caught it, no doubt, as it was contagious." How could anyone resist joining Picasso in Paris—he had just had a show given by Ambroise Vollard, a celebrated art dealer, and it seemed his career was launched. Sabartès distanced himself

Picasso and Fernande in Montmartre around 1906.

atelier was decorated when she burst into the room one summer in 1904.

Fernande became Picasso's model, as would Germaine and all of Picasso's mistresses during this time. Fernande had posed for Caolus Duran, Boldini, Rochegrosse, and (perhaps) Degas. When she met Picasso, she was living in the Bateau-Lavoir with a sculptor. The artists called her the Belle Fernande, a nickname she certainly merited. She had wild hair, green eyes, milk-white skin, and sensual womanly proportions; all this lu-

minescent nonchalance garnered her the name Odalisque. Picasso gradually pushed aside the blue that had taken hold of his work. Harlequins, acrobats, and down-and-out characters continued to haunt his canvases, but his palette lightened, from grey to pale ocher, then pink. From the moment Fernande transported her few belongings from the sculptor's atelier to Picasso's, he referred to this period of his work as "seeing the vie en rose." In spite of days of forced fasting, discomfort, and promiscuity, few were ever bored with life at the Bateau-Lavoir. Roland Dorgelés, a columnist during those pioneering days, wrote this picturesque evocation of the ambiance: "love's sighs traversed the partitions, and even more so, domestic scenes could be heard from the hatch to the hold. Then Picasso's dogs would begin to howl, Van Dongen's young daughter would burst into tears, the Italian tenor stopped singing, the man wearing the advertising sandwich board came home drunk, threatening to tear the place apart."[5]

The whole group regularly crossed the Butte to get to the Lapin Agile, recently opened by the owner, nicknamed Frédé, of the Zut on place Ravignan. This jovial bearded man never passed on an occasion to grab his guitar and sing a song. He became friendly with the ragged Spaniards who painted the walls of his bar for free. At the Zut, Pichot and Picasso tried to outdo each other's imagination—the first painted a whimsical version of the Eiffel tower, the second painted a hermit surrounded by naked women, a scene his friends encouraged him to baptize *The Temptation of Saint Antoine.*

icasso in his atelier in the Bateau Lavoir, 1908.

Frédé requisitioned Picasso to decorate the vast and somber room of the Lapin Agile. He wanted a work that would last, a frameless canvas that could be nailed directly to the wall of the cabaret. It was to hang among the bric-a-brac that included an immense mold of *Apollo with lyre,* a bas-relief copy in Javanese, and a number of poorly done paintings accepted in payment for food

and drink. Picasso's work portrayed a Harlequin standing in front of a bar holding a glass of absinthe in one hand. Behind this figure was Germaine, who had passed from the arms of the unhappy Casagemas into those of Picasso, then Pichot. She is flamboyantly dressed in the painting, but her face, white as chalk, appears as if she were wearing a mask. Life has left this immobile couple, forever frozen in waiting. Neither the strong colors, the music suggested by the presence of Frédé and his guitar, nor the liquor warm the solitude made yet more poignant by the gaiety of the surroundings—the boisterous crowd, the laughter, and merry songs. As in the painting of Sabartès in La Lorraine, alone behind his glass of beer, the Picasso-Harlequin is alone with his absinthe, the liquor that numbs the spirit to create the illusion of deceiving sadness and hunger.

For those who could spend the two francs on the menu, wine included, the Lapin Agile was satisfying, consistent, and lively. Frédé's wife, Brave Berthe, was in charge of the kitchen. She prepared appetizing meals based on the specialties of her region, Burgundy. If Picasso had already discovered beef bourguignon during his previous stays in Paris, he was now able, thanks to the credit he received in exchange for his painting, to complete his knowledge of regional cooking. The cooking at the Lapin Agile posessed the mysterious qualities Picasso had so appreciated at Els Quatre Gats. There was an abundance of charcuterie, as in

At the Lapin Agile, 1904–1905, oil on canvas. The melancholy Harlequin is actually Picasso himself standing at the bar in the Lapin Agile; Germaine Pichot, leaning on her elbow, is just behind him. A few years earlier Casagemas had committed suicide over Pichot. In the back of the room is Frédé, the owner, and his inseparable guitar.

Catalonia. Besides the traditional grilled andouillette, eaten with mustard, Berthe served a variety of pork dishes: pan-fried, with shallots, napped with white wine sauce, in a terrine marbled with chopped parsley and enrobed with a gelée that would break apart into shiny amber morsels. Thin slices of bacon filled the *crapiau*, a thick crêpe served piping hot, that could warm the harshest winter nights. Picasso, who loved omelettes and tortillas, found this dish very much to his liking.

Catalonians and Burgundians were united by their mutual passion for escargots, or baked snails. The Catalonians met on Easter Monday and Pentecost for a ritual meal of escargots in which the entire quarter participated. The snails were simply seasoned with salt and hot red pepper, and grilled over glowing vine branch embers. They were eaten with slabs of bread spread with aïoli. As for the Burgundians, they preferred their snails stuffed with softened butter blended with garlic and parsley. Regardless of these differences, a convivial ambience was established, and Picasso held Berthe's cooking in high esteem.

The painter felt very much at home at the Lapin Agile. When the weather was good he settled down with his dogs on the small terrace overlooking rue Saules. Picasso's dogs were not the only animals who frequented Frédé's cabaret—a monkey; a crow tamed by Margot, the daughter of the owner; and a donkey named Lolo all made up a sort of Noah's ark. Of course, there was also the celebrated rabbit on the restaurant insignia, that triumphantly held itself up out of a saucepan, balancing a bottle on an extended paw. The bottle might very well have been an old Burgundy marc that Frédé saved for his most faithful clients, those who were lucky enough to be held in his confidence. Several years later, the label from this bottle would be depicted in several of Picasso's cubist works.

When his credit was used up, Picasso fell back on Fernande's stews. "Although I could only spend one or two francs a day," she wrote in her diary, "Picasso's friends still appreciated my stews." In a small pan in the atelier she would sauté assorted vegetables—cabbage, carrots, potatoes, onions, and beans. On a good day, Fernande would add a nice chunk of bacon, and their friends would drop in to savor the food on the corner of the table, or on the bed, or seated on the floor as need be. When Fernande wasn't cooking, it was her friend Benedetta Canals. This beautiful Romaine had, it was said, posed for Renoir and Degas before marrying Nonell's best friend, Ricard Canals. Canals became one of Picasso's best friends, to whom he taught engraving. Their friendship grew after Picasso met Fernande, who had known Benedetta long before she entered into Picasso's life. The Canals mostly served pastas, but such wonderful pasta! Benedetta used her imagination to transform the most banal timbale into a delicious meal. She replaced ricotta and Gorgonzola, which where impossible to find, with Camembert and Brie.

above: The Lapin Agile cabaret around 1910. In front is the owner, Frédé.
Following pages: *Ham, glass, bottle of vieux marc, and newspaper*, 1914, oil and sand on canvas.

When not a penny was left, they lived on their cleverness as a last resort, as told by Fernande, "We never lunched as well at Picasso's as when we ran out of money. Our last prospect was with the pastry shop. We ordered lunch from the pastry shop on place Abbesses and asked that it be sent at exactly 12 noon. At noon the delivery person arrived, he knocked on the door in vain, as no one answered, and finished by leaving the basket of food outside the door, which we opened as soon as he left. We paid several days later when we could." If the delivery person insisted, Fernande yelled through the door, "Place it on the floor, I can not open up, I'm completely naked."

On the other hand, the door was always open to their friends. This was under the condition that they did not come by too early—that is to say, they could not call before noon. Picasso worked mostly at night, using an oil lamp, the smell of which permeated the atelier. If there was no oil left, he painted with his right hand while holding a candle in his left. There was disorder all around him. Fernande, who preferred to lie in bed reading novels, readily admitted her utter indifference toward house cleaning. When the couple could finally afford a cleaning woman "for 20 sous," she would come in and content herself to sit and savor the coffee prepared for Fernande and Pablo, who were still sleeping behind the curtain of their modest alcove. Barring the morning, the Bateau-Lavoir atelier was the place for the gang to rendezvous. It was not just for Catalonians, but all of Picasso's friends. The painter's prestige continued to grow, and his name was starting to be recognized beyond the borders of Montmartre. In 1906 he was included in a novel by Eugene

Picasso and Fernande (standing in the back) surrounded by their friends in 1907.

Vase and fruits, 1908, watercolor on paper.

Marsan. Both the work and author have since fallen into oblivion, but certainly not the artist in the book, who talks with two people in the Lapin Agile, seated in front of Picasso's self portrait as the Harlequin: "The painter of the Harlequin, as I said, had already achieved notoriety. . . . He is an Andalusian who paints, in Spanish, the look and the rag. You could call him . . . the Eye of Saltimbanques, but remember his name: Picasso."[6]

Rendezvous of the Poets

On a beautiful day in 1905, Picasso perched on his special wobbly chair and traced the following words above the door of his atelier: "Rendezvous des poètes." The use of the plural was somewhat surprising because, in spite of the title Picasso gave his portrait of Sabartès, among Picasso's gang there was only one person worthy of the rank poet, the irresistible Max Jacob. It wasn't until

a pollinaire in Yvetot, summer 1913. Four days before his twenty-third birthday, Picasso met Guillaume Apollinaire in an English bar on rue Amsterdam. The death of the poet in November 1918 broke the passionate association between the two men, who shared a love for late-night strolls around Paris, interminable discussions in cafés "full of smoke," and shapely women.

i n spring 1905 the art dealer Ambroise Vollard bought the majority of works from Picasso's "Rose Period.' Picasso used this unexpected fortune to purchase two tickets for Spain, where he spent the summer with Fernande. In a letter addressed to

[handwritten letter in French]

Carême, o Brillat Savarin
aimes-nous et quel vin pourprin
...

the painter, Apollinaire wrote about
the heroic expedition up to the train,
and the feast that preceded his departure: "O! Vatel, O! Carême, O!
Brillat-Savarin/ What dinner we had
and what wine/Flowed on the guests'
starched vests!"

above and opposite page, bottom: Front and
back of a message from Picasso to Apollinaire
before 1909. Below: Max Jacob, *Apollinaire and
his muse*, 1910, gouache on paper.

autumn 1904, a few days before his twenty-third birthday, that Picasso met the second poet of his life, not in Montmartre, but in an English pub on rue Amsterdam. The small, swarthy Andalousian found himself face to face with a giant, "an ivory figure whose chin was larger than his forehead," and who possessed a thundering laugh—Guillaume Apollinaire. At first glance they recognized each other, and immediately understood that the other was an iconoclast, and that they shared the same excessive nature.

Apollinaire abandoned the shady surroundings of the Saint-Lazare train station to become a regular on the Butte. He soon had his own napkin at the "Rendez-vous des poètes", or more accurately, his corner of a napkin. Linen was very scarce at the Bateau-Lavoir, but Fernande resolved the problem in her usual relaxed manner. "I only have one napkin," which she threw at her guests one day, "as there are four of you, organize yourselves so that each of you has your own corner." Apollinaire quickly baptized it the "napkin of the poets" which passed from hand to hand—from Juan Gris, a young Spanish painter who had recently arrived in Paris, to Max Jacob, to Apollinaire, to Picasso. Painting and poetry fraternized around Fernande's stews. The friends were surrounded by half empty tubes of paint strewn on the floor and canvases heaped up in a jumble along the walls. On some canvases, pale silhouettes of unreal, wandering entertainers sprang up. They were dressed in "lung pink" as Apollinaire, in his way, referred to the color of the acrobats' costumes in his poems.

*P*ortrait of Max Jacob in laurel wreath, **1928, pencil on paper.**

In 1905–1906, Picasso's painting style increasingly moved toward simplification. His portraits attest to this pursuit, although sometimes painfully. Even after Gertrude Stein, having recently met Picasso, posed for eighty sessions, Picasso was still not finished.

Apollinaire was not the only one to discover the path to the Bateau-Lavoir, which would not take long to become the "Acropolis of cubism," as Max Jacob referred to it. Dealers and art lovers passed by more and more frequently. They sat on the bed, or a stool borrowed from a neighbor, and flicked their cigarette ashes on the floor, as did the "maître" himself, who painted seated on the edge of the only chair in the studio, dressed in blue mechanics' overalls.

Gertrude Stein and her brother Leo crossed paths with the German Wilhelm Uhde, who, although quite fastidious, maintained his composure amid the shambles. The newcomers mixed with the regulars from way back, and even a ghost from the past returned, Ambroise Vollard, the art dealer on rue Laffitte. He had organized Picasso's first Paris exposition during the summer of 1901, but grew disinterested in the artist during his Blue Period which the dealer did not like. Apollinaire was able to convince Vollard to alter his opinion. In the spring of 1906, in front of the astonished Max Jacob and excited neighbors, the dealer carried out thirty works and put them in a carriage. These works were mostly from the Rose Period, which he immediately liked. He left behind two thousand francs, a fortune large enough for Picasso to

Restaurant, 1914, oil on canvas cut-out.

"Is the clay drier than all those torn newspapers
With which you throw yourself into dawn's conquest [. . .]
Nobly you cut out the shape of a chicken
Your hands play with your tobacco pouch,
With a glass, with a bottle . . ."
Paul Éluard

ertrude Stein in front of an enormous sequoia tree trunk in the Yosemite Park museum in California.

live on for three years. With this money Pablo and Fernande left for Barcelona and Gósol. When they returned to Paris, their everyday life improved. The couple could offer their friends true *fiestas* and banquets to celebrate the sale of his paintings, or even, as in the beginning of the winter of 1908, the purchase of a painting.

Douanier Rousseau's banquet

The money Picasso obtained from Vollard enabled him to unearth great art works himself. He often lingered in second-hand stores, the kind that offer their clientele used mattresses, chipped vases called "antiques," and modern art works, sometimes pawned by an artist in desperate straights. Such was the shabby shop of père Soulié, a former wrestler who switched to the second-hand trade. It was said he was capable of drinking up to fifty apéritifs a day. Among the art works piled up on the sidewalk across from the Médrano circus, Picasso discovered a large portrait of a woman with a hardened face. Soulié gave it to him for five francs and added, "You can even paint over it!"[7]

The painter was careful not to follow his suggestion, and prominently installed his new acquisition in his atelier. The large woman wearing a black dress was immortalized by the naïf brushwork of Douanier Rousseau. Apollinaire shared in Picasso's enthusiasm for the work, and began to write an essay on the modest Paris employee who became an artist quite out of the ordinary.

Rousseau certainly deserved a celebration. Picasso and Apollinaire rallied their friends and sent out an impressive number of invitations. Fernande was in charge of personally transmitting an invitation to Gertrude Stein and her friend Alice Toklas, an American to whom Fernande gave French lessons. In the *Autobiography of Alice B. Toklas*, Gertrude Stein tells of the preparations for this memorable party: "Fernande told me a great deal about the menu. There was to be *riz à la Valenciennes*. Fernande had learnt how to cook that on her last trip to Spain."

The rice dish was the hit of the evening. It was cooked on a neighbor's stove, so the atelier could maintain the dignity of a "receiving room." Although Fernande brought the recipe back from Spain, she failed to bring back a *paella*, the traditional two-handled flat pan that perfectly cooks the rice. She had to make due with a stock pot she borrowed that was large enough to hold rice to feed thirty or more guests. Fernande surveyed the burning coals, she left the guests ten times to check the cooking, and regularly stirred in a few ladles-full of stock to prevent the rice from sticking to the bottom of the pan or drying out. The

apple, 1909, watercolor on paper, plaster sculpture.

"It is not necessary to paint a man with a gun, an apple can be equally revolutionary." (Picasso, 1947)

hero of the evening had not yet arrived. Finally, Apollinaire appeared, ceremonially leading on his arm a small man with a goatee and large black béret. Dounanier's entrance was heralded by cheers. They could all finally go to the table. The *riz à la Valencienne,* served with rabbit, chicken, sausage, and fragrantly perfumed with saffron, was an out-and-out success. Apollinaire, always curious about the art of cooking, wanted to know the precise spice ingredients, and compared the dish to the Italian *risotto,* of which he was a great specialist.

He loudly interrupted to approve the remarks of a young painter whom he had introduced at the Bateau-Lavoir, Georges Braque. One of his paintings was placed against the wall, and there was a piece by Picasso that Apollinaire was interested in

Georges Braque, around 1912–1913.

looking at, which depicted five naked women revealing themselves. Although a rather classical subject, there was a question as to whether two of the figures were really women; they had dark, monkey-like, striated faces, sharp elbows, enormous hands, and their eyes were set askance. Braque went with Apollinaire to view the work, and neither could completely accept this new revolution from the infernal Catalan. Pablo shrugged his shoulders. Ever since he had painted the five women, who were residents of a brothel on calle Avignon, one of the more notorious streets in Barcelona, he had heard only sarcasm and criti-

cism for the work. Even Guillaume was put out. When Braque discovered the painting he exclaimed, "It is as though you want to make us eat rope or drink gasoline!"

When the cream-filled *pets-de-nonne,* small choux pastries, were served, the hour for discourse began. As Gertrude Stein recalls, "Guillaume Apollinaire got up and made a solemn eulogy. I do not remember at all what he said, but it ended up with a poem he had written, which he half chanted and in which everybody joined in the refrain, '*La Peinture de ce Rousseau.*'" Braque accompanied the chorus with the accordion. Le Douanier, blissfully happy, sampled the *pets-de-nonne,* which were coated with powdered sugar that dusted his black jacket. When it was his turn, he played a few airs on the violin from which he was rarely separated. Finally, Pichot, the sole survivor present from Els Quatre Gats, "danced a wonderful religious Spanish dance which ended in making himself a crucified Christ upon the floor."

Picasso, quiet, looked at the still life at the bottom of *Les Demoiselles d'Avignon.* It included a few of his favorite fruits as well as a slice of watermelon that was curved and tapered like the noses of the courtesans. "Pass the summer slice of melon," he wrote one day. And during this freezing early winter night in Paris, while Pichot danced in honor of Douanier Rousseau, Picasso thought of Spain.

Right Bank - Left Bank

Success had arrived. Pablo and Fernande left the Butte more and more often to dine in the heart of the city. They walked down rue Laffitte to the shop of Ambroise Vollard. The dealer received them in the basement. "A partition separated the basement in half from the shop," Vollard wrote in his *Mémoires*, "one half, aerated by the basement window, was used for cooking, the other half served as a dining room. In this room, which was closed off to the outside, the heat condensed into moisture." Vollard told the following anecdote: "Renoir, dining with me one night, asked me as he was picking up his cane which he had placed against the wall:

- Does your house have a leak?

- A leak? Where?

- Look at my cane, it's all wet . . ."

In spite of this discomfort, the basement dinners were quite lively, as witnessed by Apollinaire, "the cooking was simple but flavorful, the dishes were prepared following the principles of old French cooking still popular in the colonies, the food was cooked for a long time over a low flame, and the flavor was heightened with exotic seasonings." Vollard, born and raised in Réunion, often served curried chicken, the national dish of his native island which he "seasoned according to inspiration, to which his créole accent added a strange charm, so subtle, so agreeable!" Fernande Olivier added.

If the art dealer spared little to feed his favorite artists, he, on the other hand, did little to show their works. "If you went to Vollard's you would never find a Picasso or any of the other works that he jealously guarded and only showed to a privileged few. But what treasures there were in the basement at rue Laffitte!" Fernande remarked. There was no question—he would never divulge his greatest works to the snobs and nouveaux riches who had little appreciation for modern painting. A high-society German had heard that "Vollard's basement" was a place where one must be seen, and thought it was a night club.

The poet Paul Fort (right) on the terrace of La Closerie des Lilas in 1920. He launched the café by organizing poetry lectures to which Guillaume Apollinaire dragged Picasso.

"In truth, the basement was such that there wasn't anything to be envious of in a Montmartre cabaret," as told by the master of the house. The ambiance was warm, especially when Picasso was there. Vollard had the knack of bringing out Pablo's devastating sense of humor. One day Pablo picked up a slice of cold tongue on the pretense that it was a likeness of the dealer. The rounded top represented his head (often concealed by bérets, hats, and tied scarves in the créole style that Vollard was so fond of), and the long segment closely resembled the lines of his ape-like face. Picasso wished (and would continue to) that his host did not have the advantage he had held ever since Picasso's first exposition in 1901, which, contrary to what Vollard claimed with a certain insincerity in his Mémoires, was not a fiasco.

Some invitations took the painter and Fernande to the right bank, which they were beginning to discover. Tuesdays they had the habit of frequenting a brasserie situated on the edge of Montparnasse, La Closerie des Lilas. There Picasso met the members of a group of artists and writers baptized the *Vers et Prose*, or Verse and Prose, over which Apollinaire presided, as thundering as ever. Only the poet Jean Moréas got the better of him; his corrosive and terrorizing witticisms fascinated the regulars. "Tell me, monsieur Picasso," he asked one night, holding his renowned monocle on the young painter, "Velásquez . . . was he a good painter?" And without waiting for a response, he burst out in rude laughter. In spite of these few false notes, there was a good atmosphere in the comfortable rooms of La Closerie, compared to the Lapin Agile which was more of a dive. On summer nights they would sit until dawn under the trees on the boulevard, behind the evergreens in wooden planters that surrounded the terrace.

The other center of attraction on the left bank was at 27 rue de Fleurus, Leo and Gertrude Stein's house. From 1903 to 1913, the date of their separation, the brother and sister were the "most happy couple on the left bank,"[8] as one of their friends described them. They were one of the most eccentric couples as well, without any doubt. Wealthy, of independent means, capricious, they were successively passionate about medicine, primitive Italian art, and modern art. Apollinaire threw out a somewhat ironic sketch of "mademoiselle Stein, this American who along with her brothers and other relatives forms the most unexpected patronage in our time."

"Their barefeet fitted with sandals delphic.

"They raise towards heaven their brows scientific.

"Those sandals sometimes wronged them with the caterers and the café owners. These millionaires wanted to take in the fresh air on the café terraces on the boulevards, but the waiters refused to serve them and politely informed them that the drinks served there would be too expensive for people in sandals.

"They couldn't care less about waiters making fun of them, and calmly pursued their aesthetic adventures."

They poked around second-hand stores in the capital and visited art dealers. Leo discovered a passion for collecting that he passed on to his sister. The first Picasso they nailed to a wall in their pavilion on rue Fleurus depicted a naked young girl carrying a basket of flowers. This purchase was soon followed by many others, because the small Spaniard had won over Gertrude Stein "with eyes as alive as two large lakes" and his "violent ways," as she described him. Picasso was in turn seduced by this woman of impressive stature; her features seemed as though they were sculpted in granite, and her tone was rather imperious. She somewhat resembled the woman in black by Douanier Rousseau.

Menu, 1914, oil and sawdust on cardboard.

While Ambroise Vollard possessively hid the works of his favorite artists in his basement, the Steins, for their part, were far from miserly. Their door was always open to their friends in the arts. They gave a ritual grand dinner on Saturdays. Hélène, their maid, presided over the menu. Her specialty was soufflé, which was always welcomed by the guests. Now that fortune smiled on Picasso, Fernande continually tried to get her own maid to become equally skilled with soufflés. But as Gertrude Stein stressed, Hélène had her ways. Hélène detested Matisse who was a regular guest in the house; she did not appreciate the casual way he invited himself to dinner. "When Miss Stein said to Hélène, Monsieur Matisse will be staying for dinner tonight," Hélène responded, "In this case I will not make an omelette, but merely fried eggs. It requires the same amount of eggs and butter, but it is less respectful, and he will understand." It is not so certain that Matisse grasped the subtleties of this culinary message. Picasso, on the other hand, received all of Hélène's indulgences. She loved the voracity with which he devoured her spinach soufflé and his punctuality was rare among the Bohemian milieu. He did not very much like Matisse himself, and it made Matisse quite angry to see the Steins become attached to this "small toreador." "Mademoiselle Gertrude," he said, "loved the local color and theatrical effects. It was therefore not possible for someone of her quality to have a serious friendship with a person such as Picasso." But Gertrude Stein teased

*"Montparnasse was
a small unbridled paradise,
violent, almost insane,
but totally in keeping
with the sentiments
of the epoch."*
Joseph Kessel

dancing to the accordion in Montparnasse, photographed by Kertész in 1926.

Paris

him about his bias, and sarcastically called him "C. M.," signifying "Cher maître."

In 1908, Gertrude's lover, Alice Toklas, moved in. Her arrival inaugurated a new era of cooking in the house. Besides the French specialties and Italian recipes Stein brought back from her trips to Tuscany, there now appeared typical American dishes cooked by Alice. "I commenced to cook simple dishes that I had eaten in homes in the San Joaquin valley in California—fricasseed chicken, corn bread, apple and lemon pie. Then when the pie crust received Gertrude Stein's critical approval, I made mincemeat . . ." This tart was filled with an assortment of dried fruits, and the aroma drifted up to the atelier to those waiting in the pavilion. On Saturdays they served in the living room, as the dining room was too small and cluttered with overflowing shelves of books. Gertrude Stein was careful not to offend anyone, seating each artist in front of his art works. Matisse sat in front of his *Femme au Chapeau,* and Picasso sat facing his portrait of the hostess, which he had finally finished upon his return from Gósol the previous summer.

Alice Toklas adjusted her cooking in tune to the guests. She let her imagination be free, serving dishes to match the colors of the paintings. "One day that Picasso lunched with us, I decorated a fish in a way that I thought he would find amusing. I chose a beautiful striped bass and cooked it according to a theory by my grandmother. . . . She maintained that a fish who had passed all his life in water should never, once caught, have contact with the element in which it was born and grew up. She recommended that the fish be grilled or poached in wine, cream, or butter. So I made a court-bouillon with dry white wine, peppercorns, salt, bay leaf, a thyme branch, a little mace, an onion stuck with clove, carrot, leek, and a bouquet of herbs. All this was gently cooked in a fish pan for one hour, then cooled. Afterwards, the fish was placed on the rack and the pan was covered. The court-bouillon was gently brought to a simmer and the fish was poached for twenty minutes. Then it was left with the court-bouillon to cool. Afterward, it was carefully drained, dried, and placed on a fish platter. Just before serving, I coated the fish with plain mayonnaise and decorated it using a pastry bag and tip with red mayonnaise, colored not with ketchup—how horrifying!—but with tomato paste. Next, I made a design with hard boiled eggs pushed through a drum sieve, egg white and egg yolk separately, truffles, and chopped *fines herbs*. I was proud of my *chef-d'œuvre* when it was served and Picasso exclaimed how beautiful it was. 'But,' said he, should it not rather have been made in honor of Matisse than of me?'" The bass decorated in red and yellow was, in effect, more in keeping with Matisse's vivid canvases than those Picasso was painting at the time.

Artistic revolution and cuisine bourgeois

After Picasso's return from Horta de Ebro at the end of the summer of 1909, he and Braque, who had become his inseparable companion, threw themselves into new pursuits. Braque worked to deconstruct reality, in order to take hold of all its facets. "He scorned form, reducing all—settings, figures, and houses, into geometric outlines and cubes." These remarks by art critic Louis de Vauxcelles, made during Braque's first exposition in November 1908, could also have applied to Picasso, co-inventer of cubism.

What, then, remained of the pigeon with peas in his work of the same title? Only the essential: the suggestion of shape, with a few rounded

Pigeon with peas, 1912, oil on canvas.

curves at the center of a structure to the right, five or six marbles in shades of grays, as color was only a trap that stopped the eye at the surface of objects. Finally there is one pigeon leg standing upright; the realism is imprinted in aggressive violence. *Pigeon with peas* is emblematic of the work that his father don José had painted twenty years before and that young Pablo had fervently wished to copy himself. But this painting was neither merely a major cubist work nor a matter of settling accounts with his father—it was also a detailed reflection on the painter's new lifestyle. Pigeon with peas was one of the dishes that would from then on appear on Picasso's table. He now had a real table, real Chippendale chairs sent from Barcelona to celebrate his move, in September 1909, into a beautiful apartment on boulevard de Clichy.

Yet, in spite of the mahogany furniture, grand piano, and the maid in white apron, the room where Picasso worked was forever in shambles. It was absolutely forbidden to clean the room, for fear that the dust would land on, and stick to, still-wet canvases. Dust balls accumulated on the masks, primitive statues, bottles, and musical instruments the artist collected to break up shapes in his work. Only his faithful dog Fricka and the small monkey Monina were given complete liberty to come and go in the atelier. Monina was a favorite of the painter; she stole the fruits he used for his still lifes, smoked cigarettes, shared his food, and terrorized the guests that came on Sunday afternoons. Picasso had a day on which he received, as did all the "chic" people. "He chose Sunday, an odious day for those who did not have the constraint of working during the week," wrote Fernande Olivier. But the charm had worn thin. Max Jacob, as always, delivered his usual clowning. With his pants rolled up he imitated a lustful dancer singing Offenbach or spouting Corneille. Fernande passed around plates filled with cookies and petits-fours, but she no longer had fun for no reason, as before.

Picasso's personal life had also changed. He had met another woman, the mistress of a Polish painter and friend of Apollinaire named Louis Marcus, and called Marcoussis. The woman was named Marcelle, but Picasso called her Eva. After Picasso and Eva ran away together several times to the south of France, to Céret in Roussillon, and to Sorgues near Avignon, and after several scenes with Fernande, the new couple moved to the left bank in Montparnasse. The years in Montmartre were finished. The painter had crossed the Seine and abandoned the Butte, his youth, and poverty.

Glass of absinthe, 1914, painted and sanded bronze, absinthe strainer.

The best neighborhoods

Polish artists in 1925, at La Rotonde.

Crossroads of the "men of the future"

While Montmartre was left to be gradually invaded by tourists eager for colorful, hackneyed sights, Montparnasse became the crossroads of the artistic and intellectual life in Paris. Crossroads is truly the word, because everything transpired at the boulevard crossings of Raspail and Montparnasse, between two cafés that would become legendary, Le Dôme and La Rotonde.

The first was the refuge of the "dômiers," a group of Germans that Wilhem Uhde presided over. Though at times pompous, he had never hesitated to lose himself in the nefarious alleys of the Butte on his way to visit Picasso. Uhde became a self-made art dealer after giving up his studies in law. He began to present Picasso to a clientele of German art collectors but was supplanted by one of his compatriot "dômiers," Daniel-Henry Kahnweiler. Kahnweiler organized the first cubist exposition in November 1908 in his grey-velvet-draped gallery on rue Vignon. Uhde presented himself as a straight-laced Prussian, and Picasso denounced him in his well-known portrait of Uhde depicted with a small, tightly pinched mouth. Kahnweiler was at the same time a model of Germanic efficiency. After pulling the claws of the second-hand dealers from the Butte out of Picasso, Kahnweiler became his supporter and confident, and helped make him internationally renowned.

Across from the Dôme, the Russians gathered at La Rotonde—Bolsheviks before 1917, Whites after. Chagall, who was too poor, was rarely there, but Trotsky was a regular. He was known for his long diatribes against "bourgeois" art (which included cubism), and provoked passionate discussions and sometimes spectacular conversions, such as that of the Mexican painter Diego Rivera, who, upon returning to his country, covered the walls of Mexico with tremendous frescoes exalting the struggle of his people. Mayakovsky made a dazzling entrance at a banquet given in his honor, in resolute, futuristic verse: "Violet Paris, Paris in indigo rises up behind the windows of La Rotonde." So, in a few years, over a few square yards of pavement, crossed what Apollinaire called the "men of the Future," of

which he and his inseparable companions, Max Jacob and Picasso, were part. The three threw themselves into remote gastronomic expeditions that left a strong impression on Max Jacob: *"Polenta!* I am horrified by Italian and Spanish cooking. During the thirty years that I followed my friends Apollinaire and Picasso to all the *gargotentas peninsumares* [cheap Spanish restaurants] of Paris, I have eaten the best *malaria gangrenata* [gangrened malaria] and *poverellos*. The mere idea of *macaronata* [macaroni-gruel] makes me sick. It smelled of bad luck, the emigration of patchouli. I am forced to follow friendship for the price of *savatellone* [endless wanderings], and they did not consult my tastes, me, who only likes Breton crêpes, beef bouillon, and pré-salé lamb chops. . . . Do not speak to me of *polenta*, or do so only to make me appreci-

ate the joy of eating the vegetables in a pot-au-feu and beef tongue with mustard sauce."

In 1913, the painter and his companions moved to the eminent atelier on rue Schœlcher across from the Montparnasse cemetery. The space was cluttered with old, yellowed newspapers, shredded wallpaper, wires, and pieces of wood that Picasso used in his new art work. The collages he made during this period led to a series of sculptures based on wood, cardboard, and paper of which *le Violon* is one of the most remarkable. Often, in this work, reality remains identifiable through the use of food; a slice of sausage and a piece of bread in enamel-painted wood in *Casse-croûte*, or painted wood grapes in *Compotier aux raisins*. The food served as a reference, and to make it easier for the disconcerted spectator to absorb the newness of

Two still lifes, 1914, brown pen and ink drawings on paper (see p. 182).

The dining room of the artist, 1917, lead pencil.

the work. This is a theory Picasso formulated much later: "If you want to give nourishment . . . in painting, which is not easy to absorb for most people who don't have the organs to assimilate it, you need some kind of subterfuge. . . . As Hegel says, they can only know what they already know. So how do you go about teaching them something new? By combining what they know with what they don't know. Then they can vaguely perceive through their fog something they recognize; they think,

'Ah! I know that.' And then it is just one more step to 'Ah! I know all of that.' Then their spirit forges ahead into the unknown and they begin to recognize what they did not know before and they increase their power of understanding."[9] Neither the war, nor the death of Eva on December 14, 1915, interrupted these explorations. Nothing could stop this momentum—his art devoured all obstacles; he opened a route to cut through the chaos of history and the pain of grief.

"*The thundering and languorous horse, by the time the tapestry designers delivered the badly made carcass, was transformed into Fantômas's carriage horse. Our uncontrollable laughter and that of the special effects man convinced Picasso to leave this casual silhouette.*"

Jean Cocteau

drop curtain for *Parade*, 1917, painting attached to canvas.

In Rome, it was already spring. Baskets of flowers cluttered up the steps of the piazza di Spagna nearby; fountains shot up at each intersection; the Forum ruins crumbled under the wisteria; the cooking in the *osterie* had the flavor of happiness, such as the "pure olive oil guaranteed not to be a blend." They sautéed baby violet artichokes, one of the Romans' favorite vegetables, and cooked tiny onions with lard and bay leaf. In March, Picasso sent Apollinaire a note written on a bay leaf. It was a vestige of the "sweet smelling architecture" beautified during meals eaten in small dining rooms below street level, and decorated with hams and empty wine flasks. "The tables were adorned for the festival with flowers and fruits, and shrimps and peppers, and tomatoes, cucumbers, eggplants, and lettuces, and green and black olives in strong purples." The tablecloths and napkins were covered with designs that Picasso drew in a single line without lifting his hand. Among the crumbs and wine stains, horses sprang up, dancing under the arabesque of the whip flicked by Monsieur Loyal in his top hat. The serpent lines ran and coiled with extraordinary nimbleness, the painter drew with a burst of enthusiasm transmitted by the precocious sun, already-ripe fruits, and the presence of Cocteau, Diaghilev, and Stravinsky by his side. The Russian

P ortrait of Olga in an armchair, **1917,**

oil on canvas.

composer fascinated Picasso to the point that, for a moment, he supplanted Cocteau. They explored Rome, then Naples, where the ballets were being produced. From the slopes of Vesuvius to the second-hand shops, San Carlo Theater, the cheap restaurants in the ports, this improvised trip to Italy was truly, for Picasso, a "consecration of spring." "All the women are beautiful in Naples," he confided to his friend Guillaume, and added, "Everything is easy here." Work and love. It was so agreeable to work with friends full of imagination and ideas. Picasso's work on the curtain for *Parade* summed up the time spent around tables, where they passionately debated and joyfully designed, even on the knob of Diaghilev's cane. Horses and acrobats had wings, as did Picasso's imagination, and the blue balloon was symbolic of the perfectly full days into which a woman had just appeared. She was one of the dancers in the troupe; her name was Olga Khoklova.

"A real young lady," as the painter proudly referred to her. A woman from a good family—her father was a colonel in the imperial Russian army. Talent was not Olga's strong point, but she was endowed with an irreproachable education and exquisite grace. She was different from the women Picasso had known until then. "Careful," Diaghilev told him, "you have to marry Russian girls."[11] Picasso wrote Apollinaire in March 1917, "Pleasant would be the union/Of the artist and the ballerina. . . ."

After returning to Paris, Picasso took over a year to make a decision. But finally, on July 12, 1918 he married Olga in great pomp and ceremony at the Russian Orthodox church on rue Daru, with three poets as witnesses. Jean Cocteau stood for the bride, Max Jacob and Guillaume Apollinaire for Picasso. It was their last celebration together. In four months the Spanish flu took Apollinaire, and madame Picasso took little time to close her door to Max Jacob, whom she judged to be a "bad sort."

Caviar and petits-fours

From the day Olga entered Picasso's house, life revolved around the living and dining room. It was not that the ballerina was a highly skilled cook—she worried too much about her figure for that—but she had social ambitions to equal her recent marriage. Olga set herself up to receive in the house at Montrouge, where the painter had been living since the death of Eva, and which they quickly left—then in the apartment on rue La Boétie. The guests were hand picked, and were above all not the obscure artists who could in any way recall Picasso's humble beginnings.

ḃ *asket of fruit*, 1918, oil on cardboard platter.

Cocteau, Erik Satie, and the English critic Clive Bell would sit quietly around the mistress of the house on rue La Boétie where nothing evoked Picasso's presence. He never came into the impeccable salon to see guests. He lived on the floor above, in an apartment he transformed into an atelier. He planted his easel in what had been the living room, where "the window faced south and offered a magnificent view of the rooftops of Paris bristling with a forest of red and black chimneys, with the slender silhouette of the Eiffel tower rising in the distance between them," as recounted

by Brassaï. Picasso let his paints drip, and threw his cigarette butts on the floor as in the Bateau-Lavoir. When he "descended," it was to strut about among the dazzled guests, or to prepare to leave for one of the innumerable dinners he was always being invited to. Cocteau, who referred to Pablo as his Cher Magnifique, introduced him to high society. The whirlwind roaring twenties were in full swing.

How many buffets, collapsing under pyramids of fruit and overflowing with multicolored canapés, did Picasso stand before, holding a glass of champagne? How many tables charged with crystal and silver did he sit at, to the right of the hostess, who savored the triumph of having this

Settled in on rue La Boétie, Pablo and Olga Picasso led a hectic life, testified by the many orders addressed to the best caterers in Paris.

The dining room at rue La Boétie, 1918–1919, pencil. In the origianl
French inscription, Picasso substitutes the word *sale*, meaning "dirty,"
for *salle* (room).

"sacred monster" in her house? With how many
unknown men in smoking jackets did he exchange
brilliant paradoxes on art, repeated all around to
give others the thrill of having brushed against the
genius? Several years later, looking at a photo-
graph of himself in a toreador costume during a
masked ball, Picasso smiled and said one word,
"Comedia. . . ."[12]

Comedia; the sumptuous parties given by the
count de Beaumont in his mansion on rue Duroc
where the valets wore perukes. *Comedia*; during
one party given by a Persian prince in a château
near Paris, Stravinsky, quite drunk, unleashed a
pillow fight, which inspired Cocteau's young lover

Raymond Radiguet to write his novel *Le Bal du
comte d'Orgel. Comedia*; happiness with Olga had
finally run out despite the birth of their son, Paulo,
on February 4, 1921.

Picasso was suffocating. He transgressed his
wife's principles of order and good manners, and
installed an enormous electric train set for Paulo
right in the middle of the living room, receiving
guests on the rug on all fours. He took a sudden
dislike to the dining room that was occupied with
so many invitation dinners that they seemed more
"luxurious than luscious." To escape the con-
frontations with Olga that were becoming more
frequent, Picasso sought refuge in the kitchen of

water bottle does not kiss me on the lips, . . . so the napkin and the kitchen towels do not start to applaud."

"The grand ball within the kitchen tools" became the cruel and comical reply to all the fashionable receptions at which Picasso was the star attraction during these years. He put himself in the scene, "bowing very respectfully before all the utensils in the kitchen," just as he had bowed for the feathered duchesses and South American millionaires who hosted parties for him in their salons around Paris.

"What do you want," Picasso asked one of his biographers, "Olga loves tea, cakes, and caviar. And me? I love Catalan sausages and beans."[13] The divorce of the Horta de Ebro savage and the small, distinguished Russian aristocrat was consummated. Weary of the caviar and petits-fours, Picasso returned to his first loves.

his atelier, where he orchestrated "shocking feasts of imprisoned objects and illiterate vegetables." In the poems he began to write at the time of his rupture with Olga in 1935, the kitchen was the place where he soothed his sorrows. "As long as the chair does not come over to hit me as always so familiarly on the shoulder, and the kitchen table does not curl up in my arms, and the hot

The fruit woman

In 1917, Olga had assented to pose for her portrait only under the condition that her face could be recognized. Taking up the challenge, Picasso produced one of his great artworks. Ten

Picasso around 1928 (above), and with Sabartès, photographed by Brassaï, at Le Flore café, in 1939 (right).

Still life of lemons and oranges, **1936, oil on canvas.**

years later, at the subway exit near Galeries Lafayette, his infallible painter's eye spotted a young blond woman, athletic and serene—Marie-Thérèse Walter. "He grabbed me by the arm," she said, "and he told me, 'I am Picasso! You and I are going to do great things together!'"[14]

Marie-Thérèse was the exact opposite of Olga. She had a gift for secrecy, and was soon following Picasso's family on vacations without arousing the least suspicion. She was perfectly submissive and yielded to her lover's wildest desires. She mocked the idea of her portrait resembling her.

The flowers decoratively scattered over Olga's shawl and dress were succeeded by a profusion of fruits. Marie-Thérèse's voluptuous curves inspired Picasso to paint a series of portraits that were at the same time still lifes, painted in acidic colors. "The lemon lips," "the orange wires," "the plate filled with figs and raisins," these poetic fragments written in 1935 could have been inscribed on the canvases from preceding years. *La Grade Nature morte au guéridon* (1931) is a luxuriant riddle based on the love between the painter and his model, the fruit-woman. The curves of the fruits intertwine with numerous masculine symbols. Far from anguished, the deformation of the body and face here is synonymous with richness and jubilation. Apples and pears were the savory counterpoints to the reclining nudes; in *La Lecture*, Marie-Thérèse's face opens as a proffered fruit. Picasso found through his young mistress a fanciful side, in which fruits were subjected to strange

"He had, regardless of the notions admitted for the actual objective, reestablished contact between the object and the one who sees it, and, in consequence, thinks about it; he brought to us, in the most audacious way, the most sublime, inseparable proofs of the existence of man and the world."
Paul Éluard

Still life of a glass, 1937, oil on cardboard platter.

metamorphoses; pears became guitars and watermelon quarters, slices of summer.

On September 5, 1935, Marie-Thérèse gave birth to a girl, Maya, several months after Picasso's final separation from Olga. After many years of clandestine living, Marie-Thérèse could, in her turn, be in the forefront. But her "wonderfully terrible" lover would not permit it. He moved her and his daughter into a charming property in Tremblay-sur-Mauldre near Versailles, and made only brief visits.

Back in Paris, he more frequently abandoned the right bank for long promenades to other side of the Seine, near Saint-Germain-des-Prés, followed by the faithful Sabartès, who was back from Spain, and ready to devote himself as perpetual secretary to Picasso. Picasso returned to the café life of his younger years, dividing his time between cafés Flore and the Deux-Magots, with a certain predilection for the former, where he sat in front of his ritual mineral water (which he never drank) and discussed politics and poetry for hours.

Rue des Grands-Augustins

Picasso moved into his new atelier a few feet away from café Flore, on rue des Grands-Augustins, in the heart of a maze of alleys situated between boulevard Saint-Germain and the Seine. He rented the two top floors of a seventeenth century mansion. The attic had been used by Jean-Louis Barrault as a rehearsal hall. "It was, moreover, the actor who told Picasso that this curious premise, which quickly seduced him, was available. The immense space reminded him of the Bateau-Lavoir, for which he secretly retained a nostalgia all his life. He could make believe he was inside a boat with a gangplank, bunker, and hold."[15] Besides this obscure, propitious labyrinth that played on his memory, the house also possessed a sort of mythical radiance that enchanted the painter; it had been the Hotel Savoie-Carignan before the revolution. This antique residence was the scene for a short recitation by Balzac entitled *The Unknown Chef-d'œuvre*. "The description Balzac gave this house, of the rigid and somber staircase, bears a rather striking resemblance."[16] Picasso moved into this place of heroes—of Balzac, the painter Frenhofer, whose pain of perfection and uncompromising thirst were such that he could no longer paint, and he finished by killing himself. But Picasso accepted Frenhofer's challenge "And on the site of *The Unknown Chef-d'œuvre*, he painted the well-known chef-d'œuvre, *Guernica*."[17]

This story is somewhat obscure. Franco had imposed his fascist regime over Spain. In the summer of 1940 Picasso took refuge at Royan with Marie-Thérèse and Maya, where he witnessed the German troops entering the city. Pétain and Hitler had signed the armistice. France was under German occupation. Upon returning to Paris, the painter permanently installed himself on rue des Grands-Augustins. He shut himself up in his atelier and fiercely attacked his work.

During those bleak years, his still lifes bristled with menacing knifes and "suffocated outbursts of forks and spoons." In his kitchen, objects made an infernal racket, sounds "cooking in the cauldrons burst forth" as he wrote in 1937 in his poem *"The Dream and Lie of Franco."* Skulls appear, served on a bed of leeks, or accompanied by pitchers with blade-like angles. The armada of domestic utensils

Paris

above: photographed by Brassaï in 1939 in the restaurant Lipp.

Opposite: Drawing by Picasso and autograph of Paul Éluard on a restaurant napkin, 1945.

Paris

e buffet du Catalan, 1945, oil on canvas. There was a small restaurant at the end of rue des Grands-Augustins that was renamed Le Catalan in honor of its illustrious neighbor, Picasso, and became his spot. The small dining room was furnished with a brown side-board with baroque molding that was often depicted by the painter.

and food stands up like an ancient Greek chorus to express rage and pain. Picasso accomplished this not only on canvas, but also on paper. In 1941, to exorcise his hunger and anguish, Picasso wrote, "the first theater piece in which the characters are food." "In this piece," Kahnweiler said in his *Entretiens*, "we feel the whole of the Occupation. It is the question of always being hungry. . . ." Raymond Queneau presented this work, written during one the most difficult winters of the war, "Tuesday, January 14, 1941, somewhere in Paris, there is a man who wrote a play and the piece is

called *"Desire Caught by the Tai,"* and the hero in the play is called The Large Foot. This Large Foot is a writer and poet; he lives in an art studio with various people (nine) around him, most of which are situated at the height of the toes. The Onion, for instance and the Large Foot are in love, in love with The Tart."

With the first rays of sunlight, Picasso could be found absorbed in growing tomato plants that he cultivated on the edges of the windows of his apartment—especially after Le Catalan was raided and closed by the police. Brassaï remembered,

"Rue des Grands-Augustins, we passed in front of Le Catalan, the restaurant named by Picasso. It was closed. The other day inspectors raided the restaurant to take supplies. . . Picasso and several other regulars were caught red-handed. They were eating grilled chateaubriands, on one of the three days in the week that meat was forbidden. The restaurant was closed for a month and Picasso himself had to pay a fine."

Under more normal circumstances, the small restaurant, renamed Le Catalan in honor of its illustrious neighbor was the canteen to the painter and his circle. As in past times at the Lapin Agile, Picasso was at home here. "Nowhere," wrote Brassaï "does his conversation reach its all-out comical imagination as at the table, during a meal, surrounded by his friends. He is full of mischievous stories, gossip, recollections pour out and are sparked by plays on words, paradoxes. . . ."

When he didn't talk, Picasso drew on the paper tablecloth, with wine, mustard, or coffee ("With this," he said, "I have yellow, brown, and black.") which became the ingredients of works improvised with a brilliance that fascinated guests. Some did not hesitate to tear off these pieces of tablecloth on which, from one stain to another, the painter conjured up a fantastic bestiary. Neither the conversation nor the drawings he traced with his finger dipped in sauce or wine prevented Picasso from joining in with everything going on in the small dining room. He took part in discussions at neighboring tables, joked with the owner, took an interest in unfamiliar faces he noticed among the crowd of regulars. One day in May 1943, his eye lingered on two young women at the table of Alain Cuny, whom he knew well. Picasso rose and went over to greet the actor, who introduced his guests to him. One of the women wore a green turban that matched the color of her eyes; her name was Françoise Gilot.

eft: Paper cut from a restaurant tablecloth, 1945.
Followng pages: *Still life of fruits*, 1945, collage and charcoal on paper.

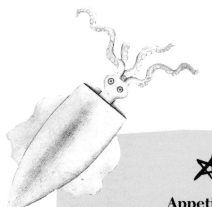

Appetizers

Soufflé Hélène
Spanish omelette
Crapiaux with bacon
(potato, cheese, and bacon fritters)
Berthe's parsleyed ham

Main Courses
Ambroise Vollard Curry
Pigeons with peas
Fernande's Rata with bacon
Valencienne rice
Sausage and beans
Macaroni gratinée
Alice Toklas's "striped" sea bass

Desserts
Chocolate Charlotte
Pears poached in wine and spices
Cream filled choux pastry
Olga's petits-fours and fruits déguisés

Soufflé Hélène

FOUR SERVINGS

3 lbs + 6 oz spinach	*1 cup milk*
5 eggs, separated	*salt and freshly ground pepper, to taste*
¼ cup butter	*nutmeg, to taste*
½ cup flour	*¼ cup grated comté° cheese*

°Any firm flavorful cheese such as cheddar can be substituted.

✻ Stem, wash, and drain the spinach. Bring a large pot of salted water to a boil. Plunge the spinach into the boiling water. As soon at the water comes back to the boil, drain the spinach and rinse it in cold water. Press the spinach between both hands to extract the excess water. Chop the spinach finely and set it aside.

✻ Preheat the oven to 450°F (240°C). Separate the eggs. Beat the egg yolks with a fork and set them aside. Prepare a roux: melt the butter in a thick-bottomed pot; add the flour and stir with a wooden spoon. In a separate pot, bring the milk to a simmer. Pour the milk into the roux, stirring constantly. Season with salt and pepper to taste. Lightly season with nutmeg. Add the grated cheese. Blend well. Slowly stir in the beaten egg yolks. Add the chopped spinach.

✻ Beat the egg whites to form firm peaks, adding salt at the beginning of beating. Fold one-third of the egg whites into the spinach mixture to lighten, then carefully fold in the remaining egg whites.

✻ Butter a soufflé mold. Fill the mold three-quarters full with the batter. Place in the preheated oven and bake for 35 minutes without opening the door. Increase the temperature to 500°F (260°C) for 5 minutes before removing the soufflé. Serve immediately.

Spanish Omelette

FOUR SERVINGS

4 potatoes	*10 eggs*
2 onions	*salt and pepper, to taste*
6 tbsp olive oil	

✷ Peel and wash the potatoes. Cut them into slices and dry them carefully. Peel the onions and slice them with the grain, across the ends. Heat half of the olive oil and sauté the onions in a large pot until they are tender and begin to brown. Add the potatoes, and sauté them for fifteen minutes, stirring often so they cook evenly on both sides.

✷ Break the eggs and place them in a large bowl. Beat them until foamy. Remove the potatoes and onions from the heat and drain them on paper towels. Place them in the bowl with the eggs, and season with salt and pepper according to taste. Combine well.

✷ Heat the remaining oil in a pan. Pour in the egg, potato, and onion mixture. Cook over moderate heat until the bottom of the omelette is set and starts to brown. Turn the omelette over and cook it on the other side while keeping the center soft and tender. Serve the potato omelette hot or cold, cut in large slices or squares.

Crapiaux au lard

(POTATO, CHEESE, AND BACON FRITTERS)
FOUR SERVINGS

9 oz bacon	*¼ cup flour*
4 potatoes	*3 eggs*
7 oz fromage blanc or sour cream	*2 tbsp butter*

✷ Cut the bacon slices into small pieces. If the bacon is salty, bring a pot of water to a boil and poach the bacon for 40 minutes at a simmer. If the bacon is not very salty, this step can be eliminated. In a second pot of water, cook the potatoes in their skins. Meanwhile, place the fromage blanc or sour cream into a bowl. Sprinkle in the flour, stirring it in. Stir in the eggs, adding them one at a time and stirring with a fork or whisk. Peel the cooked potatoes and crush them with a fork or potato ricer. Add them to the egg/flour mixture. Drain the bacon, and when cool, add it to the mixture. Season to taste. Stir until well blended.

✷ Melt the butter in a non-stick pan. Spoon 4 to 6 separate spoonfuls of the batter into the pan. Cook the crapiaux for 3 to 4 minutes, flipping them halfway through. When they are golden brown on each side, remove them to drain on a paper towel. Continue cooking the crapiaux until the batter is used up. Serve hot.

Berthe's parsleyed ham

EIGHT TO TEN SERVINGS

2 ham hocks	*1 bottle (25 fl oz) white wine*
3 carrots	*3 thyme branches*
2 onions	*2 bay leaves*
4 garlic cloves	*3 celery leaves*
4 shallots	*2 parsley sprigs*
2 veal feet	*1 leek green*
2 cloves	*salt, to taste*
20 peppercorns	*1 large bunch parsley*
nutmeg	*2 tbsp vinegar*

✳ To draw out the salt from the ham hocks, cover them with cold water and soak for 12 hours; change the water four times during this period. Peel the carrots, onions, garlic, and shallots. Drain the ham hocks and place them in a large stock pot. Add the veal feet, carrots, onions (each stuck with a clove), 3 garlic cloves, peppercorns wrapped in cheese cloth, 4 gratings of nutmeg, and white wine. Prepare a bouquet garni by wrapping the thyme, bay leaves, celery leaves, and parsley stems in the leek green, and tie with a string. Place the bouquet garni in the pot. Add enough water to just cover the ingredients. Bring to a boil, then lower the heat and simmer for three and a half hours.

✳ Meanwhile, prepare the persillade: wash and drain the parsley well, and chop it finely; chop the remaining garlic cloves and shallots and combine them with the chopped parsley.

✳ Immediately after the ham hocks and veal feet are cooked, remove them from the pot. Allow them to cool so they can be handled, then bone them. Cut the ham hocks into large, regular pieces. Finely chop the veal feet and combine with the persillade. Strain the cooking liquid, and reduce it by cooking it over a low heat for 30 minutes.

✳ In a terrine large enough to contain the prepared ingredients, alternate layers of the ham hock pieces and the veal-persillade, sprinkling each veal layer with vinegar. Pour enough of the reduced stock into the terrine to just reach the top layer. Cover with plastic wrap and place a weight on top to compact the ingredients. Refrigerate overnight. Serve from the terrine, or unmold and cut into slices.

recipes

Ambroise Vollard Curry

FOUR SERVINGS

4 onions	½ tsp ground quatre-épices
3 garlic cloves	(four spices mixture)
4 tomatoes	½ tsp ground cumin
2 apples	½ tsp ground ginger
3 tbsp vegetable oil	2 pinches powdered saffron
1 chicken, cut into 8 sections	1 small, hot red pepper
salt and freshly ground pepper, to taste	⅓ cup pineapple juice
2 tbsp powdered curry	Valencienne rice (see page 122)

✳ Peel and chop the onions and garlic cloves. Peel, seed, and chop the tomatoes and apples. Heat the oil in a pot, and brown the chicken pieces on all sides. Remove the chicken pieces and set them aside. Place the onions in the pot and cook them until translucent. Return the chicken to the pan and season with salt and pepper to taste. Sprinkle with curry, the quatre-épices (four spices mixture), cumin, ginger, and saffron. Add the tomatoes, apples, garlic, hot red pepper, and pineapple juice. Cover and cook over a low heat for 45 minutes.

✳ Towards the end of cooking, check the seasoning. Remove and discard the red pepper. Remove the chicken pieces and place them on a serving platter. Purée the cooking juices and garnishes in an electric blender. Pour the sauce over the chicken. Serve with Valencienne rice.

♦ pposite: *Pigeon with peas,* 1961, paper cut-out on terrine.

Pigeons with peas

FOUR SERVINGS

2 carrots	3 sugar cubes
2 dozen white pearl onions	2 thyme branches
3 lbs peas in the pod	1 bay leaf
2 tbsp vegetable oil	2 parsley sprigs
4 pigeons	2 celery leaves
7 oz bacon, cut into small pieces	salt and freshly ground pepper, to taste
6 lettuce leaves, sliced into thin strips	

✸ Peel the carrots and cut them into even-sized sticks. Peel the onions and keep them whole. Set the vegetables aside for later use. Shell the peas.

✸ Heat the oil and butter in a large pot. Brown the pigeons on all sides for 15 to 20 minutes. Remove the pigeons from the pot and discard the grease. Return the pigeons to the pot, add the peas, carrots, onions, bacon, lettuce, and the sugar cubes. Prepare the bouquet garni by tying together the thyme, bay leaf, parsley, and celery leaves with string, and add to the pot. Season with salt and pepper according to taste. Moisten with about 3 cups water. Cover and cook over a low heat for 35 minutes.

Fernande's rata with bacon

FOUR SERVINGS

7 oz dried white beans	*1¾ lbs slab bacon*
1 large cabbage	*2 bay leaves*
generous 1 lb carrots	*4 thyme branches*
scant 1½ lbs potatoes	*2 leek greens*
1 lb + 5 oz onions	*3 celery leaves*
4 garlic cloves	*salt and freshly ground pepper, to taste*

✯ In a bowl, cover the beans with cold water and soak for 12 hours. Drain them. Wash the cabbage, removing and discarding any tough outer leaves. Cut the cabbage into eight pieces and cut off the central core from each section. Peel and slice the carrots. Peel and cut the potatoes into quarters. Peel the onions and garlic.

✯ Place the bacon in a large pot. Cover with cold water and bring to a boil. Skim off any froth that comes to the surface. When the cooking liquid is clear, add the beans. Prepare the bouquet garni by tying together the bay leaves, thyme, leek, and celery, and add it to the pot. Season with salt and pepper according to taste. Cover and cook over low heat for one and a half hours. Add the cabbage, carrots, potatoes, onions, and garlic. Continue cooking over a low flame for one hour more. Test the seasoning and the vegetables before serving.

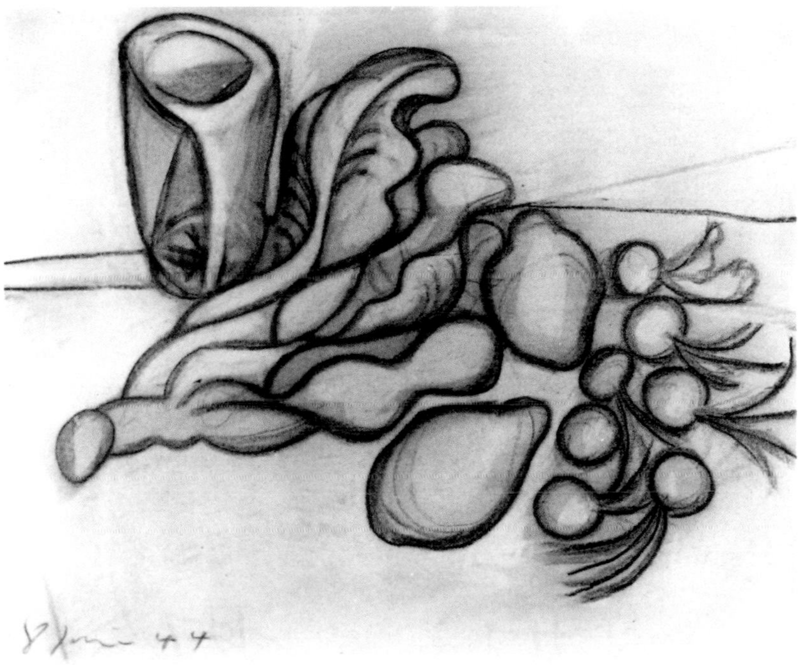

Valencienne Rice

FOUR SERVINGS

3 onions	1 tbsp paprika
2 garlic cloves	1 cup short grain rice
3 tomatoes	3 pinches powdered saffron
6 tbsp olive oil	salt and freshly ground pepper, to taste
1 small chicken, cut into 8 pieces	2 cups + 2 tbsp chicken stock
4 pieces of rabbit back	5 oz shelled peas
2 sausages	

✳ Peel and slice the onions and garlic cloves. Peel, seed, and coarsely chop the tomatoes. Heat half of the olive oil in an iron skillet, or preferably a *paella* pan. Sauté the chicken pieces, rabbit pieces, and sausages on a low heat, turning them to brown them on all sides. Remove the meat and sausage and set them aside. Discard nearly all the cooking fat, leaving just a thin layer coating the bottom of the pan. Add the onions and garlic to the pan and cook them over low heat without browning. Add the tomatoes and paprika and cook over a moderate heat for approximately 10 minutes. Return the meat and sausage to the pan. Add the rice, saffron, and salt and pepper to taste. add half of the chicken stock. Stir, and raise the heat. As soon as the stock comes to a boil, lower the flame so the stock is at a simmer.

✳ Cover and cook over a low heat for approximately 10 minutes. Add the remaining stock and the peas. Cover and cook for 10–15 minutes more. The rice should have absorbed all the stock; the chicken and rabbit should be tender. Taste to see if more salt or pepper is needed.

✳ Cover and set aside to rest for 5–8 minutes off the heat before serving.

Sausage and beans

FOUR SERVINGS

7 oz white beans	2 tbsp tomato paste
2 onions	1 cup dry white wine
1 tbsp lard	4 6-inch pork sausages
2 pinches dry thyme	salt and freshly ground pepper, to taste
2 bay leaves	

✶ Place the beans in a bowl and cover with cold water. Set aside to soak overnight. Drain off the water. Peel and slice the onions. Melt the lard in a heavy bottomed saucepan, add the onions, and cook until translucent. Add the thyme, bay leaf, tomato paste, and wine. Stir in the beans. Pour in enough cold water to cover. Add the salt and pepper according to taste. Cover and cook over a low flame for approximately 1 hour, stirring occasionally. Add the sausage and more water if needed. Cover and continue to cook over a low heat for approximately 1½ hours.

Macaroni gratinée

FOUR SERVINGS

1 tbsp coarse salt	freshly grated nutmeg
1 tbsp vegetable oil	3 tbsp butter
10 oz macaroni	3 oz grated comté°
3 oz crème fraîche or heavy cream	3 tbsp bread crumbs
3 oz grated Parmesan cheese	butter for the baking dish
Salt and freshly ground pepper, to taste	

°Benedetta Canals could not always find the Italian cheeses in Paris that she was used to using for Romaine macaroni. She substituted brie or Camembert for a somewhat surprising, but pleasing result.

✶ Bring 3 quarts water to a boil with the coarse salt and oil in a large saucepan. As soon as the water boils, add the macaroni. Cook for 8–10 minutes. The macaroni should be a little firm to the bite. Drain and discard the cooking water. Return the macaroni to the saucepan. Add the crème fraîche and half of the grated Parmesan cheese. Season with salt, pepper, and a few gratings of nutmeg. Stir well. Preheat the oven to 375°F (200°C). Butter a baking dish and add half of the macaroni. Sprinkle half the grated comté cheese on top. Cover with the remaining macaroni. Sprinkle with the remaining cheese, and dot with butter. Sprinkle on the bread crumbs. Bake until the top is golden brown, approximately 20 minutes.

Alice Toklas's "striped" sea bass

FOUR SERVINGS

Court-bouillon	*3 celery leaves*
2 onions	*1 leek green*
2 cloves	*1 pinch mace*
2 carrots	*10 peppercorns*
2 quarts white wine	*1 whole sea bass, about 3 lbs*
2 quarts water	*20 parsley sprigs*
6 parsley sprigs	*20 chervil branches*
2 tarragon branches	*1 tbsp tomato paste*
2 bay leaves	*2 cups mayonnaise*
3 thyme branches	*2 hard-boiled eggs*

✳ Prepare the court-bouillon. Peel the onions and stick a clove in each. Peel and slice the carrots. Pour the wine and water into a fish pan or other elongated pan that will accommodate the fish. Prepare the bouquet garni by tying the parsley, tarragon, bay leaves, thyme, and celery leaves in the leek green, and add it to the pan. Add the carrots, onions, and mace. Wrap the peppercorns in cheese cloth and add them to the pan. Season with salt. Cover and bring to a boil, then turn down the heat and simmer for one hour. Poach the fish in the simmering court-bouillon, covered, for 20 minutes. Turn off the heat and let the fish cool in the court-bouillon. After cooling, carefully remove the fish and drain it well. Remove the skin and fins from the fish and discard them. Place the fish on a platter. Wash and chop the parsley and chervil. Set it aside.

✳ Mix the tomato paste with half the mayonnaise, blending well. Place this mixture in a pastry bag with a medium fluted tip. Place the filled pastry bag in the refrigerator. Separate the egg yolks and whites of the hard-boiled eggs. Push first the egg white then the egg yolk through a sieve or food mill, keeping the two separate. Spread a thin layer of plain mayonnaise over the fish, omitting the head and tail if attached. Pipe out stripes of the tomato mayonnaise leaving space between each stripe. Alternate the remaining garnishes: egg yolk, egg white, and chopped herbs, filling the spaces between the stripes of tomato mayonnaise. Serve well chilled. Serve any remaining mayonnaise on the side.

Chocolate Charlotte

SIX TO EIGHT SERVINGS

7 oz unsweetened chocolate	*1 cup heavy cream*
4 eggs	*⅔ cup rum*
⅔ cup + 2 tbsp sugar	*⅔ cup water*
6 tbsp soft butter	*30 lady fingers*
4 tbsp water	

✹ Chop the chocolate and place it in a bowl. Set the bowl over a pot of simmering water.

✹ Separate the eggs. Beat the egg yolks and ⅓ cup of the sugar until thick and pale. With a wooden spoon or rubber spatula, blend the warm, not hot, melted chocolate into the egg/sugar mixture. Add the soft butter. Stir until well blended. Place ⅓ cup sugar and the 4 tbsp water in a small pot. Stir until the sugar is dissolved. Boil the syrup over low heat until thickened, approximately 8 minutes. Beat the egg whites to soft peaks. Slowly beat in half the sugar syrup. Continue beating until the egg whites have medium-firm peaks. Fold the chocolate mixture into the beaten egg whites. Beat the heavy cream to soft peaks. Gently fold it into the chocolate/egg white mixture until just blended—be careful not to overwork the batter.

✹ Butter the base and sides of a charlotte mold. Combine the rum, ⅔ cup water, and 2 tbsp sugar in a small pot and bring to a boil. Set the syrup aside to cool. Dip the lady fingers in the syrup one at a time and arrange them on the bottom and around the sides of the mold. Fill the lady finger-lined mold with the chocolate mousse. Cover with a layer of moistened lady fingers. Cover with plastic wrap. Place a plate slightly smaller than the mold on top, and place a small weight on the plate to compact the charlotte. Refrigerate for 12 hours before unmolding. Serve with coffee or chocolate crème anglaise.

am jar, charlotte, and glass, 1924, oil on canvas.

Cream-filled choux pastry

MAKES 16 FILLED PASTRIES

CHOUX PASTRY:	*PASTRY CREAM:*
1 cup water	*generous 2 cups milk*
1 pinch salt	*2 tsp vanilla sugar*
1 tbsp sugar	*6 egg yolks*
¼ cup butter	*generous ⅓ cup flour*
1 cup flour	*¼ cup confectioners sugar*
4 eggs	

✳ Preheat the oven to 450°F (230°C). Prepare the choux pastry. Heat the water, salt, and sugar, and all but 1 tbsp of the butter. As soon as the water comes to a boil, take it off the heat and add the flour all at once. Return the pan to the heat and stir the batter constantly with a wooden spoon until it no longer sticks to the spoon or the sides of the pan. Take the pan off the heat and add the eggs one at a time, beating each one in until well blended before adding the next. When all the eggs have been added and the batter is smooth, put it into a pastry bag with a medium, plain tip. Butter a sheet pan with the remaining butter. Pipe out 16 balls of batter the size of a walnut on the buttered sheet pan. Bake the choux pastries for 15 minutes, then lower the oven to 400°F (200°C) and bake for 15 minutes more. Do not open the oven during baking as the pastries could fall. After baking, set the choux pastries aside to cool.

✳ Prepare the pastry cream. Bring the milk and vanilla sugar to a boil in a saucepan. In a bowl, whisk the sugar and egg yolks until thick and pale. Add the flour, and stir until blended. Whisk the hot milk into the egg mixture. Pour the entire mixture back into the saucepan and cook it over a moderately low heat for 2 to 3 minutes, stirring constantly to prevent the cream from sticking to the bottom of the pan. After cooking, pour the pastry cream into a bowl. Sprinkle the top of the pastry cream with confectioners sugar, or brush it with butter to prevent a skin from forming. Set aside to cool. It can be set over an ice bath.

✳ When the choux pastries are cool, make a small incision in the side with the point of a pastry tip. Put the cooled pastry cream in a pastry bag with a plain, medium tip. Fill each choux pastry, through the incision, with the pastry cream. Dust the filled choux pastries with confectioners sugar, and arrange them on a serving plate.

Olga's petits-fours and *fruits déguisés*

Fruits dèguisés are candied fruits "disguised" or decorated in various ways.

Date and prune déguisés

FOR 60 FRUITS

| 30 dates | generous 1 lb almond paste |
| 30 prunes | food coloring (optional), as needed |

✷ Split the dates and prunes just enough to remove the pits. Be careful not to cut them completely in half. Discard the pits and set the fruits aside. Cut the almond paste into even cubes about half the size of the fruit. Shape each cube of almond paste into an almond shape with your fingers. Place one shaped almond paste piece inside each fruit to replace the pit. Leave the fruit partially open so the almond paste can be seen. Place each filled fruit in a paper candy cup.

✷ To color the almond paste, a few drops of red or green food coloring can be worked into a portion of the almond paste before it is shaped. Be careful to keep the colors very pale.

Cinnamon craquelines

MAKES 40 COOKIES

1¼ cup flour	5 tbsp cold water
1 pinch salt	½ cup sugar
½ cup + 6 tbsp cold butter	2 tbsp ground cinnamon

✳ Combine the flour and salt in a bowl. Add all but 2 tbsp of the butter and work it with your fingertips until the mixture resembles a coarse meal. Pour in the cold water and quickly knead the mixture with your hands until the dough comes together in a ball. Cover the dough with plastic wrap and place it in the refrigerator to rest for at least 20 minutes.

✳ Place the sugar and cinnamon in a container or bag that can be tightly sealed, close the lid and shake the container to blend the ingredients. After the dough has rested, use a rolling pin to roll it out on a cool work surface lightly dusted with flour. Roll the dough into a rectangle, to under ¼-inch thick. Trim off the ragged edges with a knife. Sprinkle the cinnamon/sugar mixture over the dough. Roll the rolling pin over the dough so the sugar mixture adheres to the dough. Tightly roll up the dough, jellyroll-style. Place it in the refrigerator for 20 minutes to rest.

✳ Preheat the oven to 400°F (200°C). Butter a sheet pan with the remaining butter. Take the roll of dough out of the refrigerator and cut it into about ¼-inch-thick slices. Place the slices, flat side down, on the buttered sheet pan, spacing them evenly apart. Bake them for 10 to 12 minutes until they are golden brown and lightly caramelized. Place them on a cooling rack.

Raspberry craquelines

VARIATION BASED ON THE CINNAMON CRAQUELINES (ABOVE).
MAKES 20 COOKIES

60 fresh raspberries	40 cinnamon craquelines
4 tbsp raspberry jam	(see recipe above)
¼ cup confectioners sugar	

✳ Stem the raspberries, if necessary. Do not wash them, as they will become too soft. Spread a thin layer of raspberry jam on half (20) of the craquelines. Cover with a second craqueline. Top each with three raspberries. Lightly dust with confectioners sugar.

Amandines with cream

MAKES 30–40 COOKIES

6 tbsp butter	*1 cup heavy cream*
½ cup sugar	*2 tbsp vanilla sugar*
1 cup almond powder	

✴ Preheat the oven to 350°F (180°C). Cream the butter and sugar. Gradually work in the almond powder. Place this mixture by teaspoonfuls in small paper candy cups. Place them on a sheet pan and bake for 15 minutes. Take the amandines out of the oven when they are golden brown, and set them aside to cool.

✴ Make sure the heavy cream is well chilled and whip it to soft peaks, adding the vanilla sugar halfway through whipping. Place the whipped cream in a pastry bag with a fluted tip and pipe a decorative rosette on top of each amandine.

Glazed apricot amandines

VARIATION OF THE AMANDINES ABOVE.
MAKES 40 COOKIES

1 lemon	*40 amandines (above)*
7 oz apricot jam	*40 blanched almonds*

✴ Squeeze the lemon to extract the lemon juice. In a thick-bottomed saucepan combine the lemon juice and apricot jam. Cook the jam until the mixture is reduced and fairly thick. Strain the jam and cook it again for 10 minutes.

✴ Spread a layer of the thickened jam on top of each amandine. Top with a skinned almond.

a bove: Picasso in 1966.

Opposite: *Plate with Fish*, 1953, painted glazed earthenware.

the midi

Paris, rue des Grands-Augustins, 1948. Three flamboyant plates are glazed in Spanish colors—ocher

and saffron. They are all alike, including "the gazpacho terrine with the bull fight." Each evokes "the sun where anchovies are fried" and a burst of tomatoes and peppers. The square white kitchen on rue des

Grands-Augustins is austere, functional, nearly empty. Picasso is excited by the three Spanish plates hanging on the wall and by the cooing of the caged pigeons and turtle doves. "I will make a work of this—that is to say, of nothing," he told Françoise Gilot. He traced a network of black lines, which he laid flat in empty space, with gaps made by three concentric circles, like targets, to represent the plates. Three birds counterbalanced the abstraction. But could a kitchen painted by Picasso, reduced to a grey surface with black lines, truly be called nothing? For those who understand the importance of the kitchen in the home, and in the painter's imagination, there is some doubt of this. Under the severe geometric grid it is possible to decipher the multiple images and blending epochs that make this canvas a riddle of his life.

This grey is the residue of the black years of the war, most of which Picasso spent on rue des Grands-Augustins. A trace of suffocation persists, as in the conclusion of the fourth act of his play "Desire Caught by the Tail," when "in the prompter's hole, on a large fire in a large pan, we saw, we heard, and we smelled the potatoes frying in boiling hot oil; the smoke from the french fries filled the theater more and more until the smothering was complete."

Birds came from farther away to traverse his works—from his childish copies of his father's paintings, to the peace dove which would, one year later in 1949, become Picasso's symbol, giving him yet more stature.

Finally, plates suspended like targets in a labyrinth indicated the new goal toward which the artist was orienting his work; he intended to concentrate a large portion of his time and creative energy from then on toward pottery. He discovered Vallauris that year. His need to create after the suffocation and forced seclusion of the war drove him to leave Paris and settle in the South of France.

above: *La Cuisine*, 1948, oil on canvas.

Opposite: Picasso hanging one of his paintings in the Grimaldi d'Antibes museum in 1951, photographed by Robert Capa.

a Galloise in Vallauris: in May 1948, Picasso and his family settled into this small, uncomfortable house. He was in his glory, about to embark on a life of "ostentatious simplicity," according to Jean Cocteau's caustic phrase.

Picasso with his son Paulo, who drove the Hispano-Suiza (top right); his grandson Pablito (right, and top left in the arms of Françoise). Picasso's dog Yan (center).

Picasso and Françoise Gilot in La Galloise, photographed by Robert Doisneau in 1952.

"Squids cooking in their ink in a saucepan and soaking in their fiery sauce."
Pablo Picasso

Still life of two octopus and two cuttlefish, 1946, glycerophtalic oil and charcoal on canvas.

In full light

Raw and cooked

With the war barely over, Picasso escaped to the Midi to regain his strength, and forget the anguish, the shortages, and the cold. And, above all, he needed to forget death, which was never so close as during those years, especially with the deportation of Max Jacob to the Drancy concentration camp in 1944.

In the summer of 1945, sunlight burst forth on the Côte d'Azur, which was overflowing with fleeing Parisians. Picasso felt reborn. Only the absence of a woman diminished his happiness. Picasso rectified this situation by convincing his new conquest, the young woman he met at Le Catalan, to join him at Golfe-Juan, where he rented her a house. This was the beginning of a euphoric period for the painter. He divided his time between the Château d'Antibes, which was at his disposal to use as an atelier, and Golfe-Juan, where Françoise Gilot was staying. Seated around the port, in the quiet of the end of the season, he indulged in an orgy of seafood. As one of the characters in "Desire Caught By the Tail" said in the eulogy, "The pungent erotic flavors of these dishes hold my depraved tastes spellbound for spicy and raw foods." While he swallowed sea urchins and shellfish, Picasso feasted his eyes on the spectacle that surrounded him. "Near the restaurant Chez Marcel in Golfe-Juan, where we ate nearly every day, was a tiny café that specialized in local seafood," Françoise Gilot recounted.

"There was a stand outside displaying the different varieties to tempt people into buying, but it was October and almost everyone had left. The only person who was tempted by the display was the woman who ran the place. She was so wide, and her café so narrow, there was hardly room enough inside for her, so she stood outside trying to drum up trade. She was not quite five feet, a very sturdy little body as broad as she was tall, with one of the coarsest faces imaginable, framed by a mass of corkscrew curls dyed mahogany and ending in a funny little pug nose that stuck out from under the visor of an outsize man's cap. Often as we were having our lunch, we saw her walking back and forth with a basket of sea urchins in front of her and a sharp, pointed knife, looking for a stray customer. Since almost no one ever showed up to lighten her load, from time to time she would dip into the basket, open up one of the sea urchins and suck in the contents so greedily that we would watch her, fascinated by the contrast between her soft, round, red face, and the spiny, green-violet sea urchins she kept bringing up to it. Four of the paintings in the Musée d'Antibes were built around the figure of this woman and the sailors that hung around the harbor. There is a portrait of the woman herself, one of a sailor eating sea urchins, and two other portraits of sailors, one dozing and the other yawning."

On October 22, 1946, while going through the inventory in the château-museum in Antibes

above: *Le Gobeur d'Oursins*, 1946, oil and charcoal on reused canvas.

Opposite: Message to photographer Sima on the back of the design *Fishes*, reproduced on page 40.

Picasso photographed by Robert Doisneau in 1952. The bakers in Vallauris called the small breads shaped like hands with thick fingers "picassos," and the painter willingly played with them.

Picasso began to feel at home again in his atelier on rue Fournas, far from family quarrels. Françoise Gilot told how he loved to repeat the story about Bernard Palissy burning his furniture to keep the kiln hot enough to bake his ceramics. Picasso always menacingly added "I would gladly have thrown my wife and my children in, if that was necessary to keep the fire going."

He felt he was far from the snobs and opportunists that usually surrounded him. He invited several friends to share his frugal existence on rue Fournas and recreated a *tertulia*, among which were the painter Édouard Pignon and his wife, Hélène Parmelin. "We lived," the latter wrote, "a monastic life, with owls, creaking floors, the chirping cricket, freezing cold water in a sink for sculpting"—in "a working atmosphere." On one of his visits to Vallauris, Cocteau made fun of the "ostentatious simplicity" of the Maître, to which Picasso superbly responded, "You have to be able to afford luxury in order to be able to scorn it."[1]

He celebrated his move to Vallauris at the Fabrique, the name he gave his atelier on rue du Fournas, with a house warming in the Provençal kitchen a few steps from the room where he worked. Hanging from the chimney at the Fabrique was a banderole painted by Pignon proclaiming, "Picasso dines chez Picasso." They sang to flamenco music to accompany the dishes as they were taken out hot from the kiln.

Rituals

Regardless of the many possible examples of simplicity, these could not stop the "legend of Picasso," which transformed the man into a sort of living god, a mythical incarnation of modern art. Even the bakers in Vallauris baptized small breads with four pointed sections resembling thick fingers as picassos; the painter invented all sorts of

P late with eggs and sausage, 1949, painted ceramic. Picasso often decorated his ceramics with still lifes in relief.

pranks by placing them at the ends of his sleeves. These regional specialty breads had been made since time immemorial, yet they suddenly became another addition to the myths that surrounded the "sacred monster." Regardless of the moments of seclusion at Fournas, he shrouded himself in rituals in his public as well as his private life.

Breakfast was one example. "Each morning," Françoise Gilot recalled, "Inès, the chambermaid, went in first, carrying Pablo's breakfast tray—café au lait and two pieces of salt-free dried toast—followed by Sabartès with the papers and mail. I brought up the rear. Pablo would always start to grumble, first about the way his breakfast was laid out on the tray. Inès would rearrange it—differently every day—to suit him, curtsy, and leave." Later, Hélène Parmelin remembered morning conversations on the bed, where they spoke of painting while brushing away crumbs from his toasts spread with honey. This moment was so important to Picasso that in May 1962 he gave Braque *Le Petit Déjeuner de Braque* (Braque's

Lunch at the house of Pierre Brune, curator for the Céret museum.

Breakfast) as a gift for his eightieth birthday—a cup of coffee with a sugar cube, a rusk, and small spoon on a saucer, all in ceramic. Like other events in Picasso's life, the ritual of breakfast unveiled the capricious egoism of a domestic tyrant, as well as the depth of the artist who regarded the instant each day began as sacred, the moment in which morning light blended with fragrances, as in the line he wrote in 1935: "The cup of coffee enamored the aroma."

The same ambiguity presided over a public ritual that occupied an essential place in Picasso's life and mythology—the corrida, or bullfight. From Nîmes to Céret, passing through Arles, Picasso cut across the Midi to watch the duel between man and death. He followed the toreadors' tracks, passionate for Luis Miguel Dominguín, and thrilled at the exploits of Conchita Cintrón. Their fight was the same as his—he was

pinned in combat facing a white canvas, like a matador in the center of the arena blinded by the sun. "A matador," he said "can never see the work of the art he is making. He can only feel what he is doing and hear the crowd's reaction to it. When he feels and knows that it is great, it takes hold of him so that nothing else in the world matters."[2]

This secret alignment of artistic creation and bullfighting inspired in "don Pablo" a maniacal respect for a series of customs. The morning before a bullfight was consecrated to "inspecting the bulls, greeting the matadors, and talking shop with the mayoral (the breeder)," as Françoise Gilot recounted. "These are all characteristically Spanish rites without which a bullfight is not a bullfight, and we had to get there well before noon; otherwise the whole day was spoiled for him. And then there was another rite. We had to sit down to a huge lunch of paella with all the friends who would come to Castel's house, the writers Michel Leiris and Georges Bataille, [. . .] and a dozen more. By that time Pablo was radiant. We were at the bullfight and everything was fine."

Picasso was jubilant with this "typically Spanish" ancestral ceremony, especially the paella. A typically Spanish dish, it was intimately tied to his distant past—the years in Catalonia, Horta de Ebro and Gósol, with Fernande at the Bateau-Lavoir, and the banquet in honor of Douanier Rousseau, forty years before. But this past was inaccessible to those who now surrounded him. Only Sabartès could truly appreciate as Picasso did the saffron-perfumed rice

Paella is a dish for large fiestas, to which everyone is invited, all friends and acquaintances, even the most distant, on a whim, a sudden impulse.

Many young women came to ask Picasso for an autograph, and immediately threw themselves at his table. He would feast in disguise, as the bullfighter of an operetta, beating his hands to the rhythm of the guitars. In a rigorous good mood, he was delighted to play with anything he could put in his hands—bottle caps became birds; potatoes became little men standing on matchstick legs, features scribbled with makeup pencils from the numerous pretty women around him. Finally, when he felt he had paid sufficient tribute to the

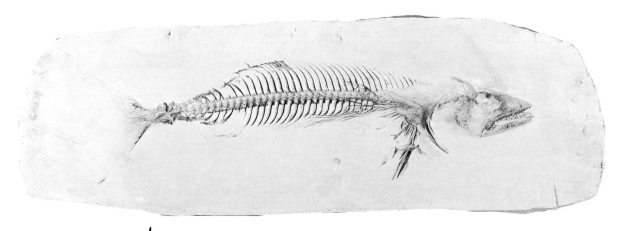

Large plaque imprinted with a fish, 1956, white molded earthenware.

for which time was one of the most important ingredients.

One day a hostess was concerned to see that Picasso had left on his plate some paella that had been made in his honor, and asked him, "Sir, you have not eaten much, was it not to your liking?" Picasso responded, "Yes, yes, Madame, there was everything. The rice, crayfish, chicken, string beans, garlic, saffron. . ." She pressed, "But then what was missing?" and he spit out the truth, "The cook, my dear Madame."[3]

devotion that surrounded him, distributing the little toys he made and good words, Picasso rose and went to the plaza to see the toros die.

Once seated he would not tolerate any distractions. One of his biographers, Pierre Cabanne, tells of this passionate aficionado's fury one day when the people seated behind him, the painter Dominguez and his wife, began to noisily eat and drink. "Pablo quickly stopped watching the corrida. Françoise, sick from the smell of the garlic sausage being devoured by their obstructive

"You the only matador.
Picassien rose and gold.
Pablo Ruiz Picasso, the bull.
And I: the picador."

Rafael Alberti, poem dedicated to Luis Miguel Dominguín

Picasso dedicating an apron to the cook at La Californie with Cathy Hutin,
Jacquelin Roque's daughter (top) looking on. The ceremony took place in front of the
linoleum-engraved poster by Picasso, *Toros en Vallauris,* for the occasion of the first
corrida organized in 1954 (center). Although they could not kill the bull (according to
French law) it was above all a reason to offer a great feast in honor of the painter (bottom).

Picasso during one of the numerous improvised festivals (top), and with Manitas de Plata (bottom), photographed by Lucien Clergue in 1968 at Notre-Dame-de-Vie.

neighbors, felt faint. Prévert spit out "stupid asses
. . ." which caused them to smother their post-
paella belching. Picasso, his eyes more black than
ever, turned toward his compatriot and addressed
him in their shared language in a torrent of abuse.
Dominguez seized the sandwiches, sausages, and
bottles of beer and threw them into the arena.
There was a moment of disbelief. But Dominguez
was Spanish and a friend of Picasso. A formidable
ovation resounded while the bullfight continued.
Pablo himself recognized that the gesture had its
appeal. The act of sacrificing food in the arena
consisted of all that pleased Picasso—the bur-
lesque of gallantry and grandiose ridicule.

For Picasso the corridas included paella lunches or copious dinners under the
thatched reeds at a restaurant with a
good ambience, or in one of the
salons of the châteaux around
Cannes. There, he was under
the same burning gazes as the
matador in the arena. He exult-
ed in the same exhilaration,
holding his listeners breathless,
hanging onto his unexpected
paradoxes, his brutal humor, his
preposterous pranks. He was
both Charlie Chaplin and
Dominguín, making small bread
rolls dance from under his
sleeves. He hid a sword of irony
under his laughter, ready to
make the final thrust at any
moment.

Other corridas, far more
cruel, unfurled in front of his
canvases and his women. By the
end of the summer in 1953,
Françoise Gilot left La Galloise
with Claude and Paloma. "No-

Standing figure, **1958, bronze.**

body before me ever did that," she said. Picasso
was actually pleased to repeat, "nobody leaves Picasso of one's own accord." The next summer
Françoise returned to bring him the children for
vacation. Picasso thought he could make her re-
gret her decision to leave. He flattered her and
tried to make her jealous. He could not understand how a woman could possibly be uninter-
ested in him.

For this project, what better place than a
corrida? Picasso had just put a few Spanish
friends in charge of organizing the first corrida
in Vallauris. He asked Françoise, under the
pretense of "one last favor," to perform the
ceremony of opening the parade. "You're
going out of my life," he said, "but you
deserve to leave with the honors of
war. For me the bull is the
proudest symbol of all, and your
symbol is the horse. I want our
two symbols to face each other
in this ritual." Françoise, a highly skilled rider, accepted the
challenge. The day of the event,
she entered the arena under the
eyes of don Pablo and Jacqueline Roque, a saleswoman from
the Madoura pottery factory,
who was seated by his side in
the place of honor.
Françoise read the proclamation
dedicating the corrida to Pablo
Picasso. It made him beam, to be
sure, to see his two rivals face to
face. But each of the women
thwarted his cruel caprice in her
own way. Jacqueline choked back
her humiliation and tears.
Françoise took a train for Paris
that night.

"When the living is good"

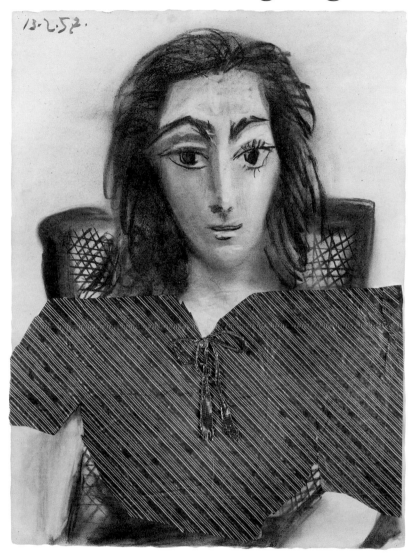

13.2.57.

*P*ortrait of Jacqueline, **1957, design with paper and glued candy-box ribbon.**

The Ogre of La Californie

Disorder again took over. The monastic austerity of Fournas and the narrow-mindedness of La Galloise was left behind. Picasso, "the king of junkmen" according to Cocteau, now reigned at La Californie, an immense residence from the end of the nineteenth century built on the Cannes heights. A many-colored tide of canvases and objects submerged the vast salons formerly belonging to the Moèt family, of the famous champagne, where they had given elegant receptions. "La Californie," Hélène Parmelin wrote, "was a mixture apart, a rationally improvised accumulation, a disorderly order, a jumble in which to know how to search, an inextricable combination of things placed where they finished their journey—some things on bottom, and others on

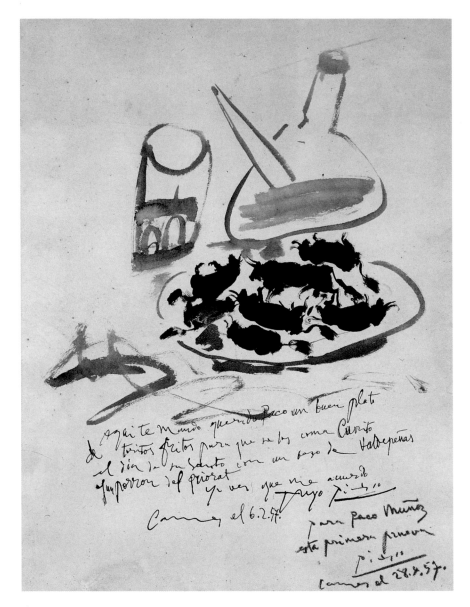

Toritos fritos, 1957, print. Picasso dedicated this large design of "little fried bulls" to the bull manager, Paco Muñoz, in celebration of the birth of Muñoz's son.

top—but we knew whose they were. They were Picasso's, naturally."

There was an epic disorder, a shambles of universal dimension. There was a pile of works, an accumulation of finds, a chaos of gifts. Everything was all over the place. There were bottles behind primitive statuettes; paints in mustard pots; mandolins suspended with hams; crayfish and smoked salmon on a marble table from Survage; Spanish, colored saltcellars were stuck among books; silver platters were propped against armchairs. The large bull heads and minotaurs Picasso had cut out were scattered about watching the labyrinth of disorder for which only the artist possessed Ariadne's clue. Nothing was in its place, yet all was in the place that the painter assigned with the improvised genius that had at other times inspired such fantastical recipes as "little Andalousian fried bread casseroles, in which bread with lard was steeped in café au lait."

If things appeared to be perpetually displaced, the places themselves were reassigned according to original function. A kitchen on the basement floor became an engraving atelier. Georges Limbour commented, "Picasso is downstairs in the basement, where the numerous rooms are well lighted from the basement windows. He works in a former kitchen; along the wall, there are four or five adjoining ovens which serve, at present, as a table. On a heavy piece of furniture set against the wall, on which, in the past cooks chopped vegetables to prepare Russian soups, he spreads the acid on the copper plaques." "Still wet" engravings came out of this former kitchen to illustrate a book on tauromaquia, written in the eighteenth century by a Spanish bullfighter, with good scenes of the corrida from Arles and Nîmes. The small, "quick and lively" bulls, similar to those in an India ink design given as a gift to a friend who raised bulls, seem to compose a strange fried dish in the hollow of a plate.

Though the basement was dedicated to engraving, everywhere else was used for painting and sculpture. Picasso wrote or designed "seated in the middle of so many hyperboles mixed with cheese and tomato," he said, "in this place inhabited by painting, which is made in silence, where it lives in permanence, where can-

vases of all ages and sculptures coexist and confront each other. Following the order of the architecture, life unfolds in the atelier, the entire atelier participates in the flesh and bone of daily life. At the bottom of it all is the canvas under way on the easel."[4]

For three years, 1955 to 1958, Picasso lived and worked in Cannes and celebrated his birthdays in Vallauris with the potters. It was as though a secret nostalgia for the house-warming at Fournas had never left him. In 1956 there was champagne and an elaborate, tiered cake from the Ramiés, the owners of the Madoura pottery. On October 25, 1957 there was a quite a banquet. On the menu was Chicken galantine, Siagne trout à l'orange, Bresse guinea hen in cream, peas in butter, new potatoes, Provençal cheeses, and a tiered cake decorated with characters made in sugar inspired by Picasso's work. The curious and voracious guests watched as the painter was given his works to taste; he devoured them, to the enthusiasm of the guests. Picasso allowed himself to be won over by this wild gourmandism; he let go of his customary frugality and inflicted his ogreish caprices on his entourage. According to Hélène Parmelin, "He had the tyranny to fill the plates of those seated next to him. He liked people to like what he liked, and would do all he could to force you to eat, and to force you to think it was good, or at least to say you did, which was the limit. He would disgustingly crush raspberries in milk and pretend

Picasso in 1961

*"The painter
pulled out his dreams
like a tooth
he finds himself
all alone
in front of the
unfinished canvas with
right in the middle
of his broken dishes
the terrifying seeds
of reality."*

Jacques Prévert

**Picasso and Jacqueline at
La Californie in 1955.**

that I must adore this because Russians only eat raspberries like this, as that was my origin, etc. He filled my plate with this mixture which was the color of grog and was indignant to see a common mortal opposed to his raspberries because it made me ill. He adored ginger and swallowed enormous pieces under my nose, offering it to me twenty times. How could I not like something so good?"

At a restaurant in the Toulon port where Picasso often sat accompanied by Jacqueline and the Pignons, he would order veal's head to which Hélène Parmelin had the same reaction as Max Jacob, when he was served polenta and pasta: "They ate enormous heaping plates. Picasso would especially order a light sauce, but he finished by eating the other as well. They shared mountains of cartilage and flabby meat. It was revolting . . . During this time, boats full of marines floated by the corolla, of young women turned, as well as the radar. Picasso began to ask if the veal's head would stay bowed down or set itself upright in his stomach. With all he said . . . I was sick to my stomach."

Vertigo sinks in, in front of the "mountains of food," the hoard of objects, and perpetual visitors. Energy was running low. Even Picasso finally acknowledged that La Californie was packed full—full of things, canvases, and people. In 1958, Picasso fled his banquet birthday given by the potters. He isolated himself in the Camargue. That year he bought the château de Vauvenargues.

The hinterland

"I've bought the Saint-Victoire," Picasso proudly announced to Kahnweiler.

"Which one?" asked the art dealer, surprised that one of Cézanne's landscapes had been on the market without his being aware of it.

"The real one," Picasso replied.

The painter now lived in the heart of a Cézanne painting. It was a château complete with secret staircases, pious relics in the chapel, and owls in the towers. "Vauvenargues," or a return to the source. The "Californian" bulimia of Cannes was followed by a dream of "secluded life" inland in Aix-en-Provence.

The light and silence was impregnated with a savory aroma of game. At the table of a small neighboring restaurant, Chez le Garde, Picasso rediscovered thrush and young wild boar pâtés, and mushroom omelettes. These were the same dishes, with similar ingredients, that Picasso remembered from the Catalonian mountains, where wild boar were plentiful in the green oak forests in which he had learned to hunt, accompanied by Josep Fontdevila who owned the inn at Gósol. Along with the pâtés and omelettes were the Catalan-style civet, or stews, for which Picasso tried to recall the recipe made with small pieces of cansalada and persillade.

"Delicious," Picasso repeated, kissing the tips of his fingers, which delighted his entourage. He savored this new life of liberty. But he could not flee the legend. He could not longer be truly free. The solar dream of Vauvenargues would not take place for him. The crowd of friends and affluent tourists that flocked to the village and the corrida were better able to retain the dream. But the people no longer enjoyed the *torero* as much, whom Picasso portrayed as impassive and unhappy in *Romancero of the Picador*—though he actually produced little during this time. In 1959, he worked on a variation of *Déjeuner sur l'herbe* by Manet, as he had two years before on *Las Meniñas* by Velázquez. According to Pierre Cabanne, he undertook to "dismember" *Le Déjeuner sur l'herbe* "to nourish his creative faculty." Picasso had dreamed of inviting Cézanne to dine, and

The chateau of Vauvenargues, photographed by Willy Ronis in 1969.

Appetizers
Brouillade in sea urchin shells
Lobster bouillon
Herb soup

Main Courses
Veal head with gribiche sauce
Jacqueline's matelote
La Galloise Sole
Grilled squid on squid ink rice
Pan-seared red snapper with anchovy sauce
Herdsman's toro
Thrush with olives
Ratatouille

Desserts
Goat cheese in olive oil
Raspberry roll
Ginger fruit soup
Honey roasted peaches
Two-tone cake

V ase with foliage and three sea urchins, 1946,
oil on paper glued to canvas.

Brouillade in sea urchin shells

FOUR SERVINGS

16 sea urchins   *salt and freshly ground pepper, to taste*
6 eggs   *12 chervil leaves*
2 tbsp crème fraîche or heavy cream

Carefully open the sea urchins using a pair of scissors, cutting around the side of the bottom or "mouth" of the shell. Turn the opened shell over and discard the water and any debris. With a small spoon, scoop out the coral. Set aside 36 pieces of the most attractive coral for garnish. Crush the remaining coral into a purée. Wash 12 of the sea urchin shells in water, then drain them. Break the eggs into a bowl. Whisk them with a fork and gradually incorporate, a little at a time, the sea urchin purée and the crème fraîche or heavy cream. Season with pepper and only a small amount of salt, as the urchins tend to be naturally salty.

Pour the sea urchin mixture into a bowl. Set the bowl over a pan of simmering water, and cook gently, stirring constantly. When the eggs are cooked, but still very tender, stir in the remaining crème fraîche or heavy cream. Spoon the mixture into the prepared sea urchin shells. Decorate the top of each filled shell with 3 pieces of coral, placing one end of each at the center to form a star. Place a chervil leaf in the center. Serve immediately.

Lobster bouillon

FOUR SERVINGS

4 small lobsters	1 celery rib
2 carrots	3 sprigs flat-leaf parsley
1 leek	2 tablespoons butter
2 shallots	1⅓ cups white wine
6 peppercorns	1⅓ cups chicken stock
6 coriander seeds	4 sprigs chervil
1 star anise	5 stems fresh coriander
zest from 1 orange	5 sprigs flat-leaf parsley
1 pinch cayenne pepper	salt and freshly ground pepper, to taste
2 thyme branches	

Rinse the lobsters in cold water. Fill a large stock pot with water and bring it to a boil. Blanch the lobsters in the boiling water for 2 minutes. Wash and cut the carrots into cubes. Wash and cut the leek into 2-inch-long, 1-inch-wide strips. Peel and finely mince the shallots. Coarsely crack the peppercorns, coriander seeds, and star anise. Place them along with the orange zest, cayenne pepper, thyme, celery, and 3 sprigs parsley into a square of cheesecloth and tie it securely.

Melt the butter in a stock pot and sweat the shallots, carrots, and leek. When tender, add the wine. Reduce the wine over a low heat for approximately 6 minutes, then add 4 cups water and the chicken stock. Add the cheesecloth packet with the seasonings. Season with salt and pepper to taste. Cook at a simmer for 45 minutes. During this time, rinse and dry the fresh chervil, coriander, and parsley. Set aside 24 chervil leaves and 8 coriander leaves. Finely chop the remaining herbs. Turn off the heat and set the bouillon aside to cool. When cool, strain the bouillon through a fine sieve. Bring the bouillon to a simmer. Taste to verify the seasoning. Put the chopped herbs in the bouillon along with the lobsters. Cook at a low simmer for 15 minutes.

Serve each lobster in a soup bowl. Cover with the herb bouillon. Divide the fresh chervil and coriander leaves among the bowls. Serve immediately.

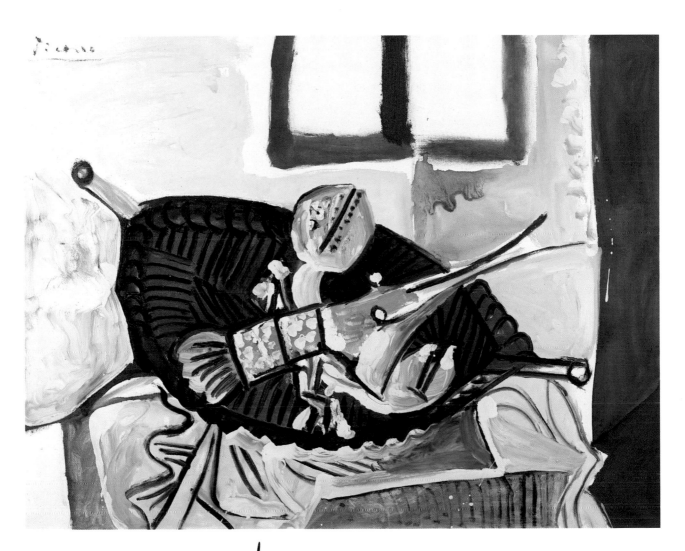

*l*obster in basket, 1965, oil on canvas.

Herb Soup

SIX SERVINGS

6 radishes	1 egg yolk
2 chervil bunches	6 small slices toast (optional)
1 sorrel bunch	salt and freshly ground pepper, to taste
2 garlic cloves	coarse sea salt, as needed
2 tbsp olive oil	

Wash the radishes, removing the stems. Set the radishes aside for later use. Wash and drain the chervil and sorrel. Reserve 20 stems of chervil, and finely chop the remainder with the sorrel. Peel the garlic cloves.

Over a low heat, heat the oil in a sauté pan. Add the garlic and chopped greens, stirring with a wooden spoon. Add 10 cups water. Season with the salt. Bring to a low boil, then lower the heat and simmer, covered, for 35 minutes. After cooking, taste to verify the seasoning, adding salt as needed. Purée the soup in a blender or food processor. Strain the puréed soup.

Whisk an egg yolk in a soup tureen, then add the soup and stir. Sprinkle the top with the chervil leaves. Serve the soup with the toasts and freshly ground pepper according to taste. Serve the radishes on the side with the coarse salt.

Veal head with gribiche sauce

FOUR SERVINGS

3 carrots	*Gribiche sauce:*
3 leeks	*3 stems tarragon*
28 oz veal head, prepared and rolled	*6 chervil stems*
2 onions	*6 sprigs flat-leaf parsley*
2 cloves	*5 chives*
3 thyme branches	*1 shallot*
2 bay leaves	*3 eggs*
4 sprigs flat-leaf parsley	*1 tsp mustard*
1 celery rib	*½ tsp vinegar*
	salt and freshly ground pepper
	to taste
	¾ cup vegetable oil
	1 tsp capers
	1 tsp cornichons

Peel and wash the carrots and leeks. Cut them in large cubes and set them aside.

Place the veal head in a stock pot. Add just enough cold water to cover. Bring to a boil, skimming off any froth that comes to the surface. Peel the onions and stick a clove in each. As soon as the cooking liquid is clear, add the carrots, leek, and onions. Prepare a bouquet garni by combining the thyme, bay leaf, parsley, celery, and peppercorns in a cheese cloth and tie it securely. Add to the pot. Salt to taste. Cover and cook at a simmer for 2 hours.

Prepare the gribiche sauce 20 minutes before the cooking is completed. Wash and drain the tarragon leaves, chervil, parsley leaves, and chives. Chop them finely. Peel and dice the shallot. Hard boil the eggs for 10 minutes in boiling, salted water. Set them aside to cool by putting them in a bowl of cold water. Shell them and separate the egg whites and yolks. Chop the egg whites finely and set them aside. Crush the egg yolks in a bowl with a fork. Stir in the mustard and vinegar. Season with salt and pepper and blend well. Briskly whisk in the oil, pouring it slowly in a fine stream, until the sauce takes on the consistency of a thick mayonnaise. Gently stir in the capers, cornichons, egg whites, shallots, and chopped herbs.

Drain the veal head and place it on a platter. Serve while hot, accompanied by the gribiche sauce on the side.

Jacqueline's matelote

FOUR SERVINGS

12 white pearl onions, with stems if possible	2 celery ribs
6 tbsp butter	2 tbsp olive oil
1 tbsp sugar	3 garlic cloves
salt and freshly ground pepper, to taste	2 lbs + 10 oz eel filet, skinned
5 oz bacon	3 tsp eau-de-vie (brandy)
2 yellow onions	1¼ cups fish stock
2 carrots	1 small bay leaf
2 leek whites	2 pinches dried thyme
	garlic croutons, as needed

☀ Peel the small white onions leaving on about ¾ inch of the green stem. Cook them in a sauté pan with the butter, sugar, three pinches of salt, and a few turns of the pepper mill. Cook, over a low heat, covered, for 25 minutes or until tender.

€ el Matelote, 1960, oil on canvas, with the following dedication: "In tribute to Jacqueline for the matelote she made for lunch on 12/3/60, and offering her with this painting just the immense desire to please her. Picasso."

Cut the bacon into ½-inch strips crosswise. Blanch the bacon in a small pot of boiling water for 15 minutes. Drain and set aside. (If the bacon is not very salty this step can be eliminated.)

Peel the yellow onions and carrots. Wash the leeks and celery. Cut all the vegetables into a fine julienne (thin strips). Heat the oil in a heavy-bottomed pot and add the vegetables, cooking them without browning. Crush the garlic and add it to the pot with the skin on. Stir occasionally, cooking over a low heat for 5–6 minutes. Cut the eel into approximately 2-inch pieces and cook them for 5 minutes, stirring occasionally. Add the eau-de-vie and flambé by tilting the pan slightly towards the flame on a gas burner or light with a match on an electric burner. Season with salt and pepper to taste. Add the wine and fish stock, then add the bay leaf, thyme, and bacon. Cook for 10 minutes over a low heat, stirring the eel pieces gently so they cook evenly. At the end of cooking, add the small white onions.

Put the eel matelote into a deep serving platter or bowl. If the cooking juices are too liquid, reduce them, after removing the eel and vegetables, over a high flame for 5 minutes. Serve with garlic croutons.

La Galloise Sole

FOUR SERVINGS

6 lbs +10 oz broad beans in shells	*1 oz butter*
3½ oz bacon	*2 pinches fresh savory*
4 whole sole, trimmed	*salt and freshly ground pepper, to taste*
flour for dredging	*3 fresh mint leaves*
4 tsp vegetable oil	

Shell the beans and put them in a large saucepan of salted boiling water. Blanch them for 30 seconds starting after the water comes back to a boil. Drain them, and immediately cover with very cold water. Remove the thick peel on the beans. Put the peeled beans in a saucepan of salted boiling water and cook them for 4 to 5 minutes. Drain them and set them aside. Cut the bacon into ½-inch strips, crosswise. Blanch the bacon in a small pot of boiling water for 15 minutes. Drain and set aside. (If the bacon is not very salty, this step can be eliminated.)

Dredge both sides of the sole in flour and pat them to remove any excess flour. Heat the oil in a large non-stick pan. When the pan is hot, put the sole in and cook them over a moderate heat for 3 minutes on each side. In a second pan, brown the bacon pieces in half of the butter for 5 minutes over low heat. Add the beans, the remaining butter, and the savory. Salt and pepper to taste. Cook for 2 minutes. Chop the fresh mint and sprinkle it over the beans.

Drain the sole on paper towels and serve them hot, accompanied by the beans.

Spanish plate with fish, 1949, painted ceramic.

Grilled squid on squid ink rice

FOUR SERVINGS

4 medium or 8 small squid   Squid stuffing:

1 onion   2 tomatoes

Squid ink rice: 2 garlic cloves

2 tbsp olive oil   10 parsley sprigs

2 tbsp butter   2 red peppers

generous 1 cup short grain white rice   2 tbsp olive oil

¾ cup dry white wine   2 tbsp pine nuts

2 cups chicken stock   salt and fresh ground pepper, to taste

salt and freshly ground pepper, to taste   4 tbsp bread crumbs

1 onion

Cut the heads off the squid, and cut the tentacles from the heads. Save the heads which contain the ink sacks. Remove and discard the beak from the center of the tentacles. Remove and discard the intestines, the transparent cartilage inside the body, and the purple membrane on the outside. Finely chop the tentacles and flippers. Pour the ink from the ink sacks into a bowl, and discard the heads. Add 2 tablespoons white wine to the ink. Set aside.

Prepare the stuffing. Peel, seed, and coarsely chop the tomatoes. Peel and chop the onions and garlic. Wash, drain, and finely chop the parsley leaves. Place the red peppers under the broiler to blacken the skin, turning them so they blacken evenly. Peel off the skin. Cut the peeled red peppers into thin strips. Set aside four attractive strips for garnish, and dice the rest. Heat half of the oil in a pan, add the onion, squid tentacles and flippers, tomato, diced pepper, garlic, pine nuts, and parsley. Season with salt and pepper to taste. Blend the mixture well. Cook over low heat for 10 minutes. Off the heat, add the bread crumbs. Fill the squid bodies with the stuffing. Seal the opening of each squid with a toothpick. Dab the squid with the remaining oil and grill them for 18–20 minutes, turning them over halfway through the cooking.

Meanwhile, prepare the rice. Peel and finely chop the onion. Heat a saucepan with half the oil and the butter. Add the onion and cook until translucent. Add the rice and cook for a few minutes until translucent, stirring with a wooden spoon. Add with the remaining white wine. As soon as the wine is completely absorbed, add the chicken stock, a ladle at a time, stirring constantly until each addition is absorbed before adding the next. All the stock should be absorbed after 15 minutes of cooking. Add the remaining butter and oil, and the squid ink and wine mixture, stirring them into the rice. Cook until the liquid is absorbed. Season with salt and pepper, remembering that the squid ink tends to be salty.

Turn the rice out onto a platter. Place the grilled squid on top. Decorate each squid with a strip of red pepper, and serve hot.

Herdsman's *toro*

MAKES 6–8 SERVINGS

3 lbs + 5 oz beef shoulder, cut in chunks	2 cloves
8 garlic cloves	20 gratings nutmeg
3 onions	salt and freshly ground pepper, to taste
4 carrots	1 bottle (26 fl oz) Côtes-du-Rhône
4 thyme branches	white wine
3 bay leaves	2 tbsp white wine vinegar
4 sprigs parsley	4 tbsp olive oil
2 celery leaves	9 oz bacon
1 piece (about 2 inches)	2 lb + 2 oz tomatoes
dried orange peel	

Place the meat on a large plate. Peel the garlic cloves, and scatter them on and around the meat. Peel and slice the onions and carrots, and distribute them in the same way. Prepare a bouquet garni by tying the thyme, bay leaves, parsley, and celery leaves with string, and place it on the meat. Scatter the dried orange peel and cloves over the meat, along with the grated nutmeg, salt, and pepper. Sprinkle the wine and vinegar over the meat. Stir and cover with plastic wrap. Refrigerate to marinate over night.

After marinating, strain off and save the marinade. Separate the meat and the vegetables. Cut the bacon into ½-inch pieces. Heat the oil in a heavy-bottomed pan and brown the bacon and the meat over a fairly high heat. When the meat is brown on all sides, add the vegetables and the marinade. Cover the pan and cook at a simmer for 3 hours. Towards the end of cooking, peel, seed, and roughly chop the tomatoes. Add them to the stew and cook for 30 minutes more.

Serve accompanied with steamed potatoes or noodles.

Thrush with olives

FOUR SERVINGS

8 thrush or quail	*1 tbsp butter*
salt and freshly ground pepper, to taste	*3 tbsp marc*
8 olive leaves	*½ cup Beaumes-de-Venise muscat*
8 thin slices lard	*9 oz sweet black olives*
2 tbsp olive oil	

If using quail, salt and pepper the interior of the birds. If thrush is used, keep the intestines inside during cooking for maximum flavor. Wrap an olive leaf over each bird (bay leaves can be substituted) then cover with a slice of lard and tie it on with butcher twine. Heat the oil and butter in a large, heavy-bottomed pan. Brown the birds on all sides. If quail are used, flambé with the marc. Add the muscat (regardless of the type of bird). Season with salt and pepper. Cover the pan and cook over a very low heat for 10 minutes. Add the olives. Continue cooking for 10 minutes longer. Check the seasoning, adding more salt or pepper as needed.

Serve the birds hot over pan-fried polenta.

Ratatouille

FOUR SERVINGS

5 medium-sized zucchini	2 onions
1 green pepper	4 garlic cloves
1 red pepper	⅔ cup olive oil
5 medium-sized eggplants	1 thyme branch
5 tomatoes	salt and freshly ground pepper, to taste

Rinse the zucchini and the green and red peppers. Peel the eggplants. Remove and discard the stems, seeds, and white membrane of the peppers. Cut the zucchini, peppers, and eggplants into a 1-inch dice. Peel, seed, and coarsely chop the tomatoes. Peel and slice the onions and garlic.

Heat 5 tablespoons of the olive oil in a large heavy-bottomed skillet over moderate heat. Add the eggplant and brown the cubes on all sides for approximately 10 minutes, stirring frequently with a wooden spoon. Transfer to a platter. Add 3 tablespoons of the olive oil to the pan. Sweat the onions and peppers over a low heat for 6 to 8 minutes, stirring frequently. Add the garlic and zucchini and cook for 10 minutes. Add the tomatoes, thyme, remaining oil, and eggplant. Season with salt and pepper.

Cover and simmer over a low heat for 35 to 45 minutes, stirring and checking the cooking occasionally, until the vegetables are almost meltingly tender. Ratatouille can be served hot or cold.

Goat cheese in olive oil

FOR A LARGE 1½ QUART JAR.
15–18 SMALL INDIVIDUAL GOAT CHEESES

5 savory branches	2 tbsp black peppercorns
6 bay leaves	1 quart (approximately) light olive oil
1 tsp anise seed	

Place alternating layers of the cheeses and savory in the jar. Add the bay leaves, anise seed, and peppercorns. Pour in the olive oil, using as much as needed to cover the cheeses and herbs.

Cover the jar and set it aside in a dark, cool place to marinate for one month before serving.

Raspberry roll

SIX TO EIGHT SERVINGS

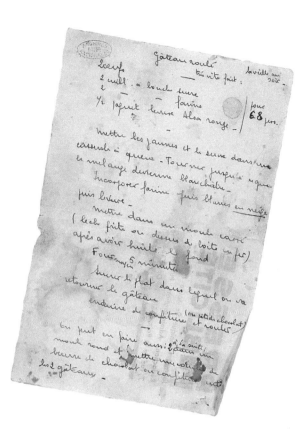

2 tbsp softened butter
scant ½ cup sifted cake flour
½ tsp baking powder
2 eggs, separated
pinch of salt
7 oz raspberry jam or jelly

The recipe for "Very-quickly-made rolled cake."

Preheat the oven to 400°F (210°C). Melt the butter over a very low heat. In a bowl, combine the cake flour and baking powder. Separate the egg whites and yolks, putting each in a bowl. Whisk the sugar into the egg yolks until they are thick and pale. Gradually and gently stir in the flour with a whisk. Add the melted butter, stirring just until the batter is blended. Beat the egg whites until foamy, add the salt, and continue beating until they hold moderately firm peaks. Gently fold one third of the whipped egg whites into the batter to lighten, then fold in the remainder, just until blended.

Line a (9 × 9-inch) square baking pan with buttered parchment paper. Pour in the batter. Bake for 5 to 8 minutes, verifying the baking as the sponge cake should not brown. After baking, cool the sponge cake before unmolding it. After cooling, unmold the cake and spread the bottom side (that which was touching the parchment paper) with the raspberry jam or jelly. Roll up the cake tightly, jellyroll-style. Wrap it snugly in aluminum foil, and refrigerate for one hour before serving.

Ginger fruit soup

FOUR SERVINGS

3-inch piece fresh stem ginger　*2 bunches white seedless grapes*
1 cup sugar　*1 small cantaloupe melon*
¼ tsp fresh lemon juice　*12 oz strawberries*
3 yellow peaches

Peel and cut the ginger into thin strips. In a small saucepan, cook the sugar and 5 tbsp water over moderate heat until it takes on a light syrupy consistency. Add the lemon juice. Add the ginger and cook it for 3 minutes. Pour the syrup into a bowl to cool.

Plunge the peaches into a pot of boiling water for a few seconds. Depending on their ripeness, this will make it easier to peel them. After peeling, cut the peaches in half and pit them. Slice the peaches. and place them in a large fruit bowl. Wash and drain the grapes. Take them off the stem and add them to the fruit bowl. Cut the melon in half and scoop out the seeds. With a medium-sized melon baller, scoop out melon balls and place them in the fruit bowl. Rinse and drain the strawberries. Stem and slice them, adding them to the fruit bowl. Pour the cold ginger syrup over the fruits and stir gently.

Arrange the fruits on top to vary the colors. Store in the refrigerator just until serving.

**Still life, 1914, pen and brown ink on paper. This piece
was part of a series of three designs (see page 92).**

Still life, 1918, oil on canvas.

Honey-roasted peaches

FOUR SERVINGS

1 ⅓ cups dry, fruity white wine
generous ¾ cup honey
8 small white peaches

2 tbsp butter
8 pinches thyme flowers (or fresh
thyme leaves)
8 lemon verbena leaves

Pour the white wine into a saucepan with ½ cup water and the honey. Bring to a boil and simmer for one minute. Preheat the oven to 350°F (180°C). Plunge the peaches into a pot of boiling water for a few seconds. Depending on their ripeness, this will make it easier to peel them. After peeling, poach the peaches in the syrup for 15 minutes, turning them around so they cook evenly. Verify the poaching with the tip of a knife; the peaches should remain slightly firm. Drain the peaches and place them in a baking dish. Moisten them with some of the syrup, and dot the top of each peach with butter and a pinch of thyme flowers. Roast the peaches for 15 minutes, basting frequently with the syrup, adding more to the pan as needed. At the end of roasting, the peaches should be lightly caramelized.

Serve the peaches warm or cold, arranged over the remaining syrup, and decorate each peach with a lemon verbena leaf. A scoop of vanilla ice cream can accompany each serving.

This recipe can also be made substituting the peaches with fresh figs.

Two-tone cake

SIX TO EIGHT SERVINGS

1 oz gelatin	*4 egg yolks*
1 cup milk	*10 oz blackcurrant jam or jelly*
1 vanilla bean	*2 cups heavy cream*
¾ cup sugar	*oil for greasing the mold*
1 pinch salt	*3 oz blackcurrants*

Put the milk and vanilla bean split lengthwise in a medium saucepan. Bring the milk to a boil. In a bowl, whisk the sugar, egg yolks, and pinch of salt until thick and pale. Take the vanilla bean out of the milk and slowly whisk the hot milk into the egg mixture. Pour the mixture into the saucepan and continue cooking over very low heat, stirring constantly with a wooden spoon, until most of the foam disappears and the mixture coats the spoon. Never allow the mixture to come to a boil. Remove the saucepan from the heat, and stir half the gelatin gently into the mixture until completely melted. Strain and set aside to cool, but do not allow it to set.

Prepare a blackcurrant mousse. Make a syrup with the blackcurrant jam or jelly and ⅔ cup water. Bring the mixture to a boil, and remove from the heat. Stir the remaining gelatin gently into the syrup until completely melted. Strain the mixture and set it aside to cool, but do not allow it to set.

Whip the heavy cream to soft peaks. Fold half of the whipped cream into the crème anglaise mixture, and the other half into the blackcurrant mousse. Oil the sides of a jello mold or soufflé dish. Pour the blackcurrant mousse into the mold, then cover with the vanilla cream.

Cover the terrine with aluminum foil or plastic wrap. Refrigerate for 6 hours. Just before serving, unmold the two-tone cake onto a serving plate and decorate with blackcurrants.

Cake on a plate, 1960, pencil on notebook paper, bearing the
dedication: "for Lionel Pregger. His friend Picasso."

List of Works

Apollinaire, poem, May 29, 1910. Picasso Archives, Musée
Picasso, Paris. (Repr. p. 74–75)

Max Jacob, *Apollinaire and his muse*, [1910], gouache on
paper, 21.5 x 15.5 cm. Musée des Beaux-Arts, Orléans.
(Repr. p. 75)

(Initial numbers refer to page numbers.)

8. *Woman carrying bread*, Gósol, 1906, oil on canvas, 100 x
69.8 cm. Philadelphia Museum of Art, gift of Charles E.
Ingersoll, Philadelphia.

9. *Picasso, Angel Fernandez de Soto and Sebastian Junyer at
the café*, Barcelona, c. 1903, ink on paper, 13.2 x 9 cm.
Museu Picasso, Barcelona.

10–11. *El Mas del Quiquet*, Puerto de Horta, summer 1898,
oil on canvas, 27 x 40 cm. Museu Picasso, Barcelona.

12. (bottom left) *Lola cutting a cake*, Barcelona, c. 1899,
pencil on paper, 33 x 23 cm. Museu Picasso, Barcelona.

(bottom right) Note dated January 19–20, 1936, Musée
Picasso, Paris.

13. (top) *The Kitchen*, Malaga, 1896, oil on wood, 9.9 x 15.5
cm. Museu Picasso, Barcelona.

(bottom) Illustrated letter to Gaby Lespinasse, February
1916, watercolor and ink on paper, 17.5 x 15.3 cm.
Collection of William McCarty-Cooper.

15. *Casas de Horta*, Horta, 1898–1899, study in pencil on
album paper, 16 x 24 cm. Museu Picasso, Barcelona.

19. *Still life of a porrón*, Gósol, 1906, gouache and
watercolor on paper, 32.5 x 37.5 cm. Private collection.

20. Letter from Pablo Picasso and Fernande Olivier to
Guillaume Apollinaire, Gósol, June 21 or 22, 1906.
Musée Picasso, Paris.

22–23. *Still life with bread*, Paris, winter 1908–1909, oil on
canvas, 60 x 73 cm. Musée National d'Art Moderne,
Centre Georges Pompidou, Paris.

24. Draft for the menu for the restaurant Els Quatre Gats,
Barcelona, [1899–1900], pen and brown ink, 32 x 22
cm. Musée Picasso, Paris.

25. Printed menu for Els Quatre Gats, Barcelona,
[1899–1900], recto and verso, 21.8 x 32.8 cm. Museu
Picasso, Barcelona.

26. *Picasso at Els Quatre Gats*, c. 1902, pen on paper, 16 x
11 cm. Museu Picasso, Barcelona.

27. *Portrait of Jaume Sabartès,* [Barcelona, 1900],
watercolor and charcoal on paper, 50.5 x 33 cm. Museu
Picasso, Barcelona.

28. *Portrait of Carlos Casagemas*, Barcelona, 1899–1900, oil
on canvas, 55 x 45 cm. Museu Picasso, Barcelona.

30. Postcard to Guillaume Apollinaire, Cadaquès, [July 5,
1910]. Picasso Archives, Musée Picasso, Paris.

35. *Picasso and Sebastian Junyer on the way to Paris*, Paris,
1904, ink and colored pencils on paper, 22 x 16 cm, from a
series of five drawings. Museu Picasso, Barcelona.

37, 113, 163. *Cuttlefish*, [1914], lead pencil on cut-out paper,
29.1 x 17.5 cm. Musée Picasso, Paris.

40, 142. *Fish*, recto and verso, Antibes, October 21, 1946,
pencil on paper, 44 x 47 cm. Collection of Marina
Picasso (inv. 4708), Jan Krugier Gallery, Geneva.

56. *Bread and fruit bowl on a table*, 1909, oil on canvas, 164
x 132.5 cm. Oëffentliche Kunstsammlung Basel,
Kunstmuseum, Bâle.

59. *Picasso and Junyer arrive in Paris*, Paris, 1904 (cf. p. 35).

60, 61. Letter to Miguel Utrillo, Paris, June 1901, pen and
colored pencils on paper, 17.5 x 23 cm. Private
collection, Geneva.

64. *Portrait of Ambroise Vollard*, c. 1907, etching, 34.8 x
24.8 cm. Musée Picasso, Paris.

65. Two pages of sketch pad number 106, c. 1908, pencil on
paper, 20 x 13.5 cm. Musée Picasso, Paris.

68. *At the Lapin Agile*, Paris 1904–1905, oil on canvas, 99 x
100.3 cm. Private collection, New York.

70–71. *Ham, glass, bottle of vieux marc, and newspaper*,
Paris, [spring 1914], oil and sand on canvas, 38.5 x 55.5
cm. Musée d'Art Moderne de la Ville de Paris, Paris.

73. *Vase and fruit, "Mort aux rats"* (sic), Paris, spring 1908,
watercolor on paper, 62.5 x 48 cm. Estate of the artist.

74–75. Note to Apollinaire, recto and verso, before 1909,
Picasso Archives, Musée Picasso, Paris.

76. *Portrait of Max Jacob in laurel wreath*, 1928, pencil on paper, 28 x 21 cm. Musée des Beaux-Arts, Orléans.

77. *Restaurant*, Paris, spring 1914, oil on cut-out canvas, 37 x 49 cm. Estate of the artist.

79. (top) *Apple*, [1909], watercolor on paper, 22 x 25 cm. Private collection, Paris.

(bottom) *Apple*, 1909, plaster, 11.5 x 10 x 7.5 cm. Musée Picasso, Paris.

80–81. *Landscape of labels*, Sorgues, summer 1912, oil and enamel on canvas, 46 x 61 cm. The National Museum of Art, Osaka.

85. *Menu*, Paris, spring 1914, oil and sawdust on cardboard, 29.5 x 38 cm. The Hermitage, St. Petersburg.

89. *Pigeon with peas*, Paris, January–March 1912, oil on canvas, 64 x 54 cm. Musée d'Art Moderne de la Ville de Paris, Paris.

90. *Glass of absinthe*, 1914, painted and sanded bronze, absinthe strainer, 21.5 x 16 x 6.4 cm. Musée National d'Art Moderne, Centre Georges Pompidou, Paris.

92, 182. *Still lifes*, Avignon, fall 1914, pen and brown ink on a yellow base on paper, .38 x .49 cm. Musée Picasso, Paris.

93. *The dining room of the artist*, Montrouge, December 9, 1917, pencil on paper, 27.7 x 22.6 cm. Musée Picasso, Paris.

94–95. Drop curtain for *Parade*, 1917, painting attached to canvas, 1060 x 725 cm. Musée National d'Art Moderne, Centre Georges Pompidou, Paris.

97. (left) *Portrait of Guillaume Apollinaire wounded*, 1916, pencil, 48.8 x 30.5 cm. Private collection.

98. *Portrait of Olga in an armchair*, Montrouge, fall 1917, oil on canvas, 130 x 88.8 cm. Musée Picasso, Paris.

99. *Basket of fruit*, 1918, oil on cardboard platter, 47.5 x 61.5 cm. Private collection.

101. *The dining room at rue La Boétie*, Paris, 1918 or 1919, pencil, 27.7 x 22.6 cm. Musée Picasso, Paris.

103. *Still life of lemons and oranges*, 1936, oil on canvas, 54 x 65 cm. Musée National d'Art Moderne, Centre Georges Pompidou, Paris.

104–105. *Still life of a glass*, April 3, 1937, oil on cardboard platter, 20 x 25 cm. Private collection.

106, 109. Drawings on a paper napkin, probably made at the restaurant Le Catalan, Paris, 1945. Collection of Myrtille Georges-Hugnet.

108. *Le buffet du Catalan*, May 30, 1945, oil on canvas, 80 x 100 cm. Musée des Beaux-Arts, Lyon.

110–111. *Still life of fruit*, 1945, collage and charcoal on paper, 21.5 x 32.5 cm. Collection of Marina Picasso (Inv. 4659), Jan Krugier Gallery, Geneva.

119. *Pigeon with peas*, March 8, 1961, paper cut-out on terrine. Collection of Lionel Prejger.

121. *Still life*, June 8, 1944, charcoal on paper, 50 x 65 cm. Musée Picasso, Paris.

127. *Jam jar, charlotte, and glass*, 1924, oil on canvas, 54 x 65 cm. Musée National d'Art Moderne, Centre Georges Pompidou, Paris.

129. *Fruits and goblet*, 1914, pencil on paper, 18.5 x 24 cm. Collection of Marina Picasso (Inv. 1846), Jan Krugier Gallery, Geneva.

131. *Still life of cookies*, Avignon, summer 1914, pencil on paper, 30 x 48 cm. Musée Picasso, Paris.

135. *Plate with fish*, August 5, 1953, glazed earthenware, diam. 32 cm. Musée Picasso, Paris.

136. *La Cuisine*, Paris, November 9, 1948, oil on canvas, 175 x 252 cm. Musée Picasso, Paris.

140–141. *Still life of two octopus and two cuttlefish*, October 1946, glycerophtalic oil and charcoal on canvas, 33.5 x 46 cm. Musée Picasso, Antibes.

143. *Le Gobeur d'Oursins*, Antibes, October 1946, oil and charcoal on reused canvas, 139.5 x 81 cm. Musée Picasso, Antibes.

144. (top) *Plate with eggplant*, 1949, decoration engraved and painted on ceramic, 32 x 28 cm. Musée Picasso, Antibes.

(bottom) *Plate with melon on gridded background*, 1949, decoration engraved and painted on ceramic, 32 x 38 cm. Musée Picasso, Antibes.

145. *Fish on a sheet of newspaper*, c. 1957, painted ceramic and clay pressed against the register of Nice's newspaper, *Le Patriote*, 39 x 32 cm. Private collection.

147. *Plate with eggs and sausage,* 1949, relief on painted ceramic, 32 x 38 cm. Musée Picasso, Antibes.

149. *Large plaque imprinted with a fish,* 1956, molded earthenware, 19 x 58 x 1.5 cm. Collection of Marina Picasso (Inv. 58 162), Jan Krugier Gallery, Geneva.

152. *Standing figure,* 1958, bronze, 125 x 47 cm. Private collection.

153. *Portrait of Jacqueline,* 1957, collage with paper and candy-box ribbon, 51 x 57 cm. Private collection.

154. *Toritos fritos,* April 28, 1957, print, 75 x 59.5 cm. Private collection.

164. *Vase with foliage and three sea urchins,* Antibes, October 21, 1946, oil on paper glued to canvas, 46 x 38 cm. Musée Picasso, Antibes.

167. *Lobster in basket,* January 10, 1965, oil on canvas, 89 x 116 cm. Private collection.

170–171. *Eel Matelote,* December 1960, oil on canvas, 89 x 116 cm. Private collection.

172. *Spanish plate with fish,* April 10, 1957, painted red earthenware, diam. 42 cm. Galerie Sassi-Milici, Vallauris.

176. *Sole and rouget platter,* [1949], fish painted and engraved in ceramic, 38 x 28 cm. Musée Picasso, Antibes.

183. *Still life,* 1918, oil on canvas, 16 x 22 cm. Collection of Marina Picasso (Inv. 12 190), Jan Krugier Gallery, Geneva.

185. *Cake on a plate,* November 30, 1960, pencil on notebook paper, 20 x 26 cm. Collection of Lionel Prejger.

Selected Bibliography

Brassaï. *Conversations avec Picasso*. Paris: Gallimard, 1969.

Cabanne, Pierre. *Le Siècle de Picasso*. Paris: Denoël, 1975.

Daix, Pierre. *La Vie peintre de Pablo Picasso*. Paris: Le Seuil, 1977. (*Picasso: Life & Art*. New York: Harper Collins, 1993.)

Dorgelès, Roland. *Bouquet de Bohême*. Paris: Albin Michel, 1989.

Ferrier, Jean-Louis. *Picasso, la déconstruction créatrice*. Paris: Terrail, 1993.

Gilot, Françoise and Carlton Lake. *Vivre avec Picasso*. Paris: Calmann-Lévy, 1965. (*Life with Picasso*. New York: Doubleday, 1989.)

Olivier, Fernande. *Picasso et ses amis*. Paris: Stock, 1993.

Parmelin, Hélène. *Voyage en Picasso*. Paris: Christian Bourgois, 1994.

Penrose, Roland. *Picasso: His Life & Work*. University of California Press, 1981.

Richardson, John. *Vie de Picasso*. Paris: Chêne, 1992. (*A Life of Picasso: Volume 1, 1881–1906*. New York: Random House, 1991.)

Sabartès, Jaume. *Picasso, portraits et souvenirs*. Paris: Louis Carré, 1946.

Stassinopoulos Huffington, Arianna. *Picasso, créateur et destructeur*. Paris: Le livre de Poche, 1991.

Stein, Gertrude. *Autobiographie d'Alice B. Toklas*. Paris: Gallimard, 1990. (*Autobiography of Alice B. Toklas*. New York: Randon House, 1990.)

Stein, Gertrude. *Picasso*. New York: Dover, 1984.

Toklas, Alice B. *The Alice B. Toklas Cookbook*. New York: Harper Collins, 1986.

Vollard, Ambroise. *Recollections of a Picture Dealer*. New York: Dover, 1978.

Notes

Quotations that are not referenced in the text are extracts taken from: Pablo Picasso, Écrits, Paris, Gallimard/RMN, 1989.

SPAIN

1. Jaume Sabartès, Picasso, portraits, et souvenirs.
2. Pierre Cabanne, Le Siècle de Picasso.
3. Le Carnet catalan, published in facsimile in 1958.
4. Jean-Louis Ferrier, Picasso, la déconstruction créatrice.
5. John Richardson, Vie de Picasso.
6. Jaume Sabartès, *Picasso, portraits, et souvenirs*.
7. Josep Pla (1897–1981) produced one of the most important works in the Catalan language; he knew numerous artists, and most notably was a friend of the surrealists.

PARIS

1. Raynal, "Panorama de l'œuvre de Picasso," Le Point, vol.7, no. 42 (Oct. 1952).
2. Charles Baudelaire, "Les Bienfaits de la lune," Le spleen de Paris. Paris: Flammarion, 1987.
3 and 4. Fernande Olivier, Picasso et ses amis.
5. Roland Dorgelès, Bouquet de Bohême.
6. Eugène Marsan, Au pays des Firmans. Paris: Société d'Éditions artistiques, 1906.
7. Roger Shahuck, in John Richardson, Vie de Picasso.
8. James R. Mellow, in John Richardson, Vie de Picasso.
9. Françoise Gilot and Carlton Lake, Vivre avec Picasso.
10. Pierre Cabanne, Pablo Picasso, His life and times. New York: W. Morrow & Co., 1977.
11 and 12. Jean-Paul. Crespelle, Picasso, les femmes, les amis, l'œuvre, Paris: Presses de la Cité, 1967.
13. Gertrude Stein, Autobiographie d'Alice B. Toklas.
14. Marie-Thérèse Walter, in Farrell, "His women," Life, Dec. 12, 1968.
15 and 16. Brassa—, Conversations avec Picasso.

THE MIDI

1. Antonina Vallentin, Pablo Picasso Paris: Albin Michel, 1957.
2. Interviews with Françoise Gilot, in Arianna Stassinopoulos Huffington's, Picasso, créateur et destructeur.
3. Interviews with the hairdresser Arias, 1994.
4. Hélène Parmelin, Voyage en Picasso.
5. Pierre Daix, La Vie de peintre de Pablo Picasso.
6. Including all quotations to the end of the chapter, Hélène Parmelin, *Voyage en Picasso*.

Index of Recipes

Spain

Paris

The midi

Acknowledgments

We gratefully thank all who contributed to the realization of this book.
Special thanks to:

M. E. Arias; The Association of Friends of the Picasso Museum at Antibes,
and Mrs. Danièle Bourgois; Mr. and Mrs. Philippe Condroyer;
Mr. André Gomès; Mrs. Myrtille Hugnet; Mrs. Cathy Hutin-Blaye;
Jan Krugier Gallery in Geneva, and Mrs. Evelyne Ferlay;
Mr. Manuel de Muga; Mr. Claude Picasso; the Picasso Museum in Paris,
Mrs. Sylvie Fresnault and Mrs. Jeanne Sudour; Mrs. Maria Teresa Ocaña,
Director of the Picasso Museum in Barcelona, and Mrs. Margarita Serrer;
Mr. Lionel Prejger; Mr. Edward Quinn; Mrs. Maya Ruiz-Picasso;
Ms. Michèle Richet; Mrs. Angela Rosengart; Mrs. Inès Sassier;
Mr. Javier Vilato.

First published in the United States of America in 1996 by
Rizzoli International Publications, Inc.
300 Park Avenue South, New York, NY 10010

First published in France in 1996 by
Éditions Albin Michel, S. A.

Copyright © 1996 Éditions Albin Michel, S. A.

ISBN 0-8478-1969-8
LC 96-67704

Translation:Rhona Lauvand
Iconography: Janine Herscher
Lay-out: Jacqueline Housseaux
Design: Rampazzo & Associés
Separation: Intégral, Paris

Printed and bound in France by Mame Imprimeurs, Tours

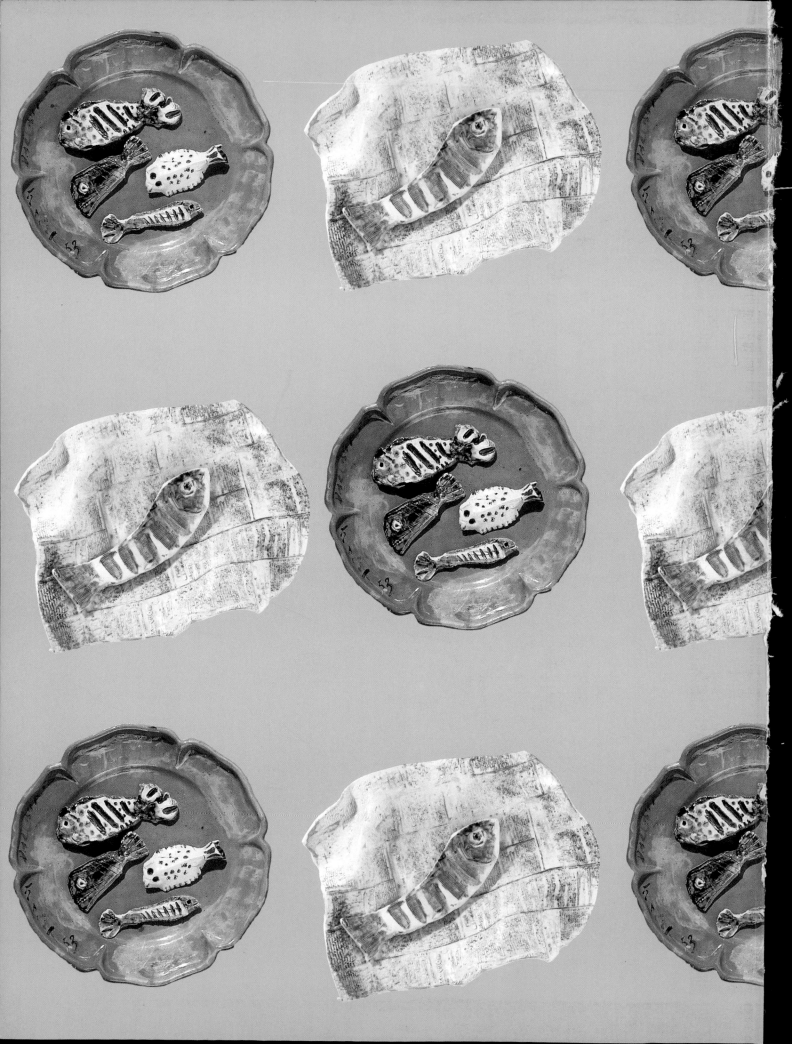